FOR EVERYTHING
A SEASON

Richard Hall

THE UNITED REFORMED CHURCH

First published 1986 by United Reformed Church, 86 Tavistock Place, London, WC1H 9RT

Illustrations by Bernard Thorogood

Typeset and printed by The Campfield Press

Contents

Foreword

To the question, 'Where were you born?' Topsy in *Uncle Tom's Cabin* replied, 'Never was born! . . . I 'spect I grow'd.' That seems to be the truth about this book. It began when I was asked to lead a Ministers' Quiet Day as a stand-in. I decided to take the theme of 'The Seasons', and as a result someone mentioned it to the Editor of *Reform* who asked if I thought a book could come from what I had prepared. I worked on an outline and chapter, half hoping that would be the end. However, I was encouraged to go further and, though the main theme remains, the book has 'grow'd' and I offer it as a book of reflections arising from a long and varied ministry, the Musings of a Superannuated Moderator.

Friends will recognise bits of sermons and echoes of discussions and conversations. I have included a number of quotations, most of which have said something to me over a long period of years. I have tried to note where they came from but in a few cases I only have scraps of paper or old sermons where they were written and I do not recall the source. I apologise for any wrongful use or misquotation.

In the hope that the book might be of greater help in personal devotions and in discussion groups I have added some questions for discussion and a few prayers, together with extensive notes which include biblical references so that the comments in the text can be carried further.

I have so many friends to thank for the help I have received in my ministry. If I were to single out one particular encouraging group it would be the members of the Emmanuel Church, Cambridge, 1952-65, who in seasons of joy and sadness helped me to see more clearly what it is to be a Christian and also a Christian church.

Richard Hall

For Everything a Season

For everything there is a season, and a time for every matter under heaven:

a time to be born, and a time to die;

a time to plant, and a time to pluck up what is planted;

a time to kill, and a time to heal;

a time to break down, and a time to build up;

a time to weep, and a time to laugh;

a time to mourn, and a time to dance;

a time to cast away stones, and a time to gather stones together;

a time to embrace, and a time to refrain from embracing;

a time to seek, and a time to lose;

a time to keep, and a time to cast away;

a time to rend, and a time to sew;

a time to keep silence, and a time to speak;

a time to love, and a time to hate;

a time for war, and a time for peace.

What gain has the worker from his toil?

I have seen the business that God has given to the sons of men to be busy with. He has made everything beautiful in its time; also he has put eternity into man's mind, yet so that he cannot find out what God has done from the beginning to the end.

The words of the Preacher, Ecclesiastes 3:1-11

When it is evening, you say, 'It will be fair weather; for the sky is red.' And in the morning, 'It will be stormy today, for the sky is red and threatening.' You know how to interpret the appearance of the sky, but you cannot interpret the signs of the times.

The words of Jesus, Matthew 16:2, 3

ONE

For Everything a Season

The seasons meant little to me when I was young. I grew up in an inner suburb of London, with only a small concrete backyard for a garden. The days of the year varied in length and there were changes in temperature. Occasionally flowers were brought into the house but as a boy I could not watch the flowers growing year after year. As I grew older I sometimes went to the local park and saw something of the changes in nature. Later, opportunities came to go out walking in the countryside of Kent and Surrey, and when I became a minister I served in Sussex during the second world war and came to appreciate not only the wonder of the physical seasons but how much we depended upon them. Years afterwards among the colleges of Cambridge I loved to see matchless spring flowers along the Backs. Now in retirement in Suffolk (a county all too little known and appreciated for its beauty) I can rejoice in the magnificence and liveliness of a spring blossoming after all had seemed dead in a severe winter, and look forward to the warmth and loveliness of summer with its time for exploration and discovery. So the seasons have increasingly meant more to me and have spoken not only of the physical changes and necessities but of the experiences and meanings of life. The very word 'season' has extended in range. In two places I have noticed this width of meaning.

What the Dictionary Says

The number of meanings given to the word in the complete *Oxford Dictionary* is too great for quotation, but in the *Concise Oxford* we have definitions such as:

Proper time, favourable opportunity, time at which something is plentiful or in vogue or active; time of year when plant flourishes, or animal breeds or is

1

hunted; time of year regularly devoted to an activity (eg cricket season) or to social activities generally; time of year when a place most frequented. Period of indefinite or various length (eg season ticket). Division of the year with distinguishable characteristics of temperature, rainfall, vegetation, etc.

I quote this to show something of the range of uses of the word 'season' but at first I shall keep to the last of these definitions, the Four Seasons of the Year, and then I shall look at other uses and see how the meanings interpenetrate each other. If we ask what each season has to say to us we will discover with Henry Thoreau, in Italy:

> The day is an epitome of the year. The night is the winter, the morning and evening are the spring and fall, and the noon is the summer.

What Ecclesiastes Says

While the dictionary definitions will be at the back of my mind, I am more concerned with the way in which a reading of Ecclesiastes 3 has for me extended the meaning of times and seasons. This Old Testament book is not generally thought of as one of the most cheerful and we do not look to it for Christian teaching. In his One Volume commentary William Neil regards the writer as possibly a man of sober turn of mind who lived in a society which was in a parlous state and who saw the cruelty and contradictions of life.[1] He thought of life as fixed with set times which came round and round. There is very little we can do about it. In the words of R. C. Walton:

> Human activity has the same fixed and pre-ordained pattern as has nature (3:1-8). Whatever God has made is unalterable, and no new factor can emerge to give a different direction to existence.[2]

Here is a picture of times and seasons which must be accepted, where good and bad are inseparable and probably of equal length. An interesting footnote to the passage in the *Jerusalem Bible* says, 'Half man's occupations are ill-omened, half his activities have to do with sorrow. Death casts its shadow on life.' I am not pursuing the gloom of this statement but I hope to catch the beauty of the thought in the final words of the passage:

I have seen the business that God has given to the sons of men to be busy with. He has made everything beautiful in its time; also he has put eternity into man's mind, yet so that he cannot find what God has done from the beginning to the end.

As a Christian I believe that this last statement can only be partially true, since God has made himself known and we can see what he has done in the physical seasons but much more in Christ. I shall be showing how the seasons help us in that understanding. We shall see this in particular as we trace the four seasons of the year, day and night, the Seasons of our Faith and the varying times and seasons of our own lives. The note will be of optimism more than pessimism. Indeed there are those who would agree with a commentator on Ecclesiastes who wrote:

Too often the whole cast of the book has been determined by certain pessimistic elements, ignoring just as patent constructive elements. . . . Chapter three has often been interpreted as a lament of the ceaseless round of life. Instead it is part of the basic optimism of Koheleth (ie Ecclesiastes).[3]

Against this background I am going to speak of what the seasons are in themselves, what they say to us and how appropriate the divisions may be. Yet often we cannot see the appropriateness. It is no part of my purpose to suggest that all life is neatly organised and that we have just the right amount of weeping and laughing, mourning and dancing, loving and hating, war and peace. That is too easy a distinction, though it is valuable to read carefully through this passage from Ecclesiastes and as we look at the manifold seasons ask what each says to us. The writer is not only suggesting

3

that there is a pre-ordained order but that there are appropriate times for being born and dying, keeping and casting away, and so on.

Inappropriate Times

For ourselves things often seem to happen out of season when we cannot see their relevance. A book to which I have continually turned over many years is John Baillie's *A Diary of Readings*, with daily passages gathered from the wisdom of many centuries. I once went through it and noted for myself a number of telling phrases and quotations. One comes from a prayer suggested by J. P. de Caussade:

O Lord, while I do not wish to neglect anything of what thou ordainest for me, for the good of my soul or my body, I hope that in due time and place thou wilt grant me the thought, the movement, and the facility to undertake and carry out such and such things which come so often and *at such inappropriate times* to present themselves to my spirit.[4]

At such inappropriate times. We often feel that God's timing is all wrong. We are not ready for the opportunity or the loss. If only something had happened at a different time! This is the wrong season. How much happier we should have been if we had known about it earlier or later! We would have been successful, we would have excelled. But it has been as it was, and a part of our need is to learn to adjust ourselves to the inappropriate seasons. I recall how I felt when asked to leave a local church where I was happy and fulfilled, to become a provincial moderator. I had plans of my own, probably to remain where I was for a few more years and then seek a less demanding pastorate before retirement. If I had been called several years previously to this new kind of ministry, it would have seemed a more appropriate timing to me. God knew better than I, and in the event I believe the 'inappropriate season' proved to be a part of God's appropriateness.

Sometimes it will seem to us that all seasons are

4

outside ourselves. They are as fixed as Ecclesiastes suggests. Spring, summer, autumn, winter—we cannot create them. Day and night—they move on regardless of anything we can do. There are seasons of faith and of experience that come to us as given from outside. Yet in fact they are not always rigidly separated. We realise that when we look at the four seasons. I began writing at a time when spring was returning after winter and there was uncertainty about each day's weather. The seasons interpenetrate and they may be adjusted to, as any night worker knows. And while I shall begin with the seasons which seem to be outside ourselves and beyond our control, there are also those which we create or encourage, times of hard work, of study, of faith and of worship.

I propose to look at the seasons in separation, to ask, for example, what spring or autumn has to say to us, but all the time I am conscious that we must see the seasons as a whole. We shall never understand our climate if we only have winter in mind. We shall never express and experience our faith fully if we are concerned only with Christmas and its message. We cannot see the truth of a life if we think only of its youth or its maturity. We must judge the whole. In trying to estimate what life has meant to a particular person I am often held back because while I knew him in his adult life, I knew little of his childhood or of the struggles of his early years. Indeed there is in most cases no one who has known the friend he remembers throughout his life. People move away, they find fresh interests, old friends die, new friends are made. No one knows the whole. Yet the man or woman whom we would recall lived a total life, through all seasons. Browning saw this in Rabbi Ben Ezra:

Grow old along with me!
The best is yet to be,
The last of life, for which the first was made:
Our times are in his hand
Who saith 'A whole I planned,
Youth sees but half; trust God: see all nor be afraid.'

So we are to think together about the many seasons of the year and of life as a whole. Some of them come but once and there is no repetition. Often I shall return to the same theme from different points of view, believing that in all the fixed and changing seasons God speaks to us and guides us. My starting point is often the passage selected from the book of Ecclesiastes, and while I make no attempt to comment on the book as a whole or to study thoroughly the passage concerning times and seasons, I hope we can see something of the writer's attitude to life. This is not easy, for all passages of the book have been discussed in detail and often scholars tell us that the phrases and apparent antitheses of chapter 3 do not mean exactly what we understand by them today. A good example is 'A time to keep silence, and a time to speak'. Is there any good reason for putting the importance of silence first? Is this how God made us? Ecclesiastes returns to the thought later:

> Be not rash with your mouth, nor let your heart be hasty to utter a word before God, for God is in heaven, and you upon earth; therefore let your words be few.[5]

This is concerned with worship; in the book of Ecclesiasticus, the injunction to keep silence is enforced in a more general way:

> A wise man will be silent until the right moment, but a braggart and fool goes beyond the right moment. Whoever uses too many words will be loathed, and whoever usurps the right to speak will be hated.[6]

Take note, all of us who frequent synods and assemblies!

It has in fact been suggested that at this point the writer is speaking of the silence of sorrow in a time of mourning and that the time to speak is the season when there is the utterance of joy after the period of mourning. This may be so but we are more likely to see here a reminder that it is better to begin in silence (and this could be when there is mourning) and then to speak when we have reflected and have something worthwhile saying.

But let us turn to the seasons that roll round with the year, to the necessary rhythm of life.

The Rhythm of Life

While the earth remains, seedtime and harvest, cold and heat, summer and winter, day and night, shall not cease.

Genesis 8:22

Thine is the day, thine also the night;
thou hast established the luminaries and the sun.
Thou hast fixed all the bounds of the earth;
thou hast made summer and winter.

Psalm 74:16, 17

To awaken each morning with a smile brightening my face; to greet the day with reverence for the opportunities it contains; to approach my work with a clean mind; to hold ever before me, even in the doing of little things, the Ultimate Purpose toward which I am working; to meet men and women with laughter on my lips and love in my heart; to be gentle, kind, and courteous through all the hours; to approach the night with weariness that ever woos sleep, and the joy that comes from work well done— this is how I desire to waste wisely my days.

Thomas Dekker

God who spoke in the beginning,
forming rock and shaping spar,
set all life and growth in motion,
earthly world and distant star;
he who calls the earth to order
is the ground of what we are.

Fred Kaan (*New Church Praise*, No 33)

In the fresh curiosity of childhood and in the leisurely contemplation of old age we are more fascinated by the eternal miracle of the seasons than in the thrust and scurry of our work in middle life.

A. J. Wavell, Introduction to *Other Men's Flowers*
selected by Lord Wavell

TWO

The Rhythm of Life

In Genesis 8:22 we are told how God proposed to deal with the terrible muddle of the world after the Flood. There would always be repeated seasons of the year and of the day. This theme is constant in the Bible. In Leviticus 23 we read of the rhythm of specially appointed days and feasts, and there will be a seventh day of rest in every week. God is therefore thought of as having built a rhythm into life so that it is always dependable. Rhythm and dependability are essential to living. Whatever be the heights to which we may soar in thought and action we must ourselves respond to that rhythm. Even if life seems dull through repetition we cannot escape this rhythm. Norman Goodall once described how he early learned this when he had to meet his ordinary duties; as a young man in a City Treasurer's Department:

> I am convinced that vocational peace in any sphere involves coming to terms with life's chores whether demanded of us by the larger operations of society or arising from the nature of all creative work, especially in that supreme creative calling of home and family life.[7]

Much of daily work and living echoes this need for rhythm and if it were not there we should find ourselves making it. There is a delightful character in Osbert Sitwell's poem *Mrs Hague*. She was the gardener's wife and

> ... swelled with ideas and ideals of duty,
>   Emphatic,
>   Rheumatic.
> For Mrs Hague was childless,
> And so had wisely broken up her life
> With fences of her own construction,
> Above which she would peer ...

For
Monday was Washing Day,
Tuesday was Baking Day,
Wednesday h'Alfred 'as 'is dinner h'early,
Thursday was Baking Day again,
Friday was a busy day, a very busy day,
And Saturday prepared the way for Sunday,
Black satin bosoms and a brooch,
A bonnet and a Bible.
These fences made life safe for Mrs Hague;
Each barrier of washing, mending, baking
Was a barricade against being lonely or afraid.
This infinite perspective
—The week, the month, the year—
Showed in the narrow gaps
Between her and the door,
As she stood there in the doorway,
Narrow as a coffin.

I quote this so fully because while it emphasises the dangers of too narrow a life of habit, it also brings out the fact and the necessity of rhythm. For everything there is a season.

The Four Seasons

We trace this rhythm in the seasons of the year. We jest about them, we complain, we greet them. We are glad when one of the seasons passes but we know it will come again and to this we look forward. The Bible so describes the farmer:

Behold, the farmer waits for the precious fruit of the earth, being patient over it until it receives the early and the late rain.[8]

A poet of this century tells how we look forward with mixed feelings:

Through winter-time we call on spring,
And through the spring on summer call,
And when abounding hedges ring
Declare that winter's best of all;
And after that there's nothing good
Because the spring-time has not come.[9]

For many people *spring*, the first full season of the year, is the most delightful. You need not be an expert gardener or horticulturist to appreciate its wonder, as indeed is true of all the seasons. We rejoice as we look at a flower slowly opening up though we are ignorant of its name. We listen with wonder as we hear the song of the birds though we cannot remember which bird it is. These tell us of the revival of the spring. Or we read the words of the poets. As I was beginning to write on this theme I discovered a delightful anthology called *Four Seasons* by Edward Phelps and Geoffrey Summerfield,[10] and as I read old favourites, and pieces new to me, more of the delight of the seasons came home. I shall often turn to it. To poetry we may add the music of the seasons. Even if you read this book in the autumn you may recall the glory of a spring day when life was being renewed after the dullness of winter. Spring is a kind season and we can understand why some think of it as the loveliest. A South African friend once told me that the spring meant more to him because they had nothing quite like it at home; their spring was so brief. So stand still, look at the flowers, listen to the music of awakening nature, feel the lift of Easter-time. It is true that sometimes spring seems long in coming but how we rejoice when it bursts upon us and once more life is vigorous. . . .

As for *summer* we never know exactly when it begins and we argue about the date of midsummer. We declare that it always goes too quickly and we often say that we have had no summer at all. Yet strangely it is the sunshine and the warmth of summer that we remember most. What of those long summer days you once enjoyed? Yet it is an ambivalent season. There is so much work to be done in the summer. Recall the farmer's care. How long are the hours and how many that you must spend in the garden. Everything grows so rapidly. But it is also the time of holiday, of sport, of visiting, and how lovely are those days! Phelps and Summerfield say that it is the time of the year when the Protestant work ethic is at its weakest.[11] Most of us are glad to be lazy and count the days to our holiday and keep recalling it. It is a time for

11

optimism, when preachers dare to choose for the coming
Sunday worship:

> Summer suns are glowing
>   Over land and sea,
> Happy light is flowing
>   Bountiful and free;
> Everything rejoices
>   In the mellow rays;
> All earth's thousand voices
>   Swell the psalm of praise.
>
> God's free mercy streameth
>   Over all the world,
> And his banner gleameth
>   Everywhere unfurled;
> Broad and deep and glorious
>   As the heaven above,
> Shines in might victorious
>   His eternal love.[12]

Often it is an unfortunate choice, since it is cloudy, wet,
even chilly, but somehow the very worst summer day still
calls for rejoicing.

Autumn has a beauty all its own and I am frequently
astonished at the glorious colouring of trees and gardens
and along the lanes. The sun may shine brightly, though
for a shorter time each day and with decreasing power.
We have all heard it described as a 'season of mists and
mellow fruitfulness'.[13] It is the season of the completion
of harvest and so one of the most valued periods. Our
churches often have their largest congregations at this
time as the people gather to thank God for his faith-
fulness once more. Ye there is a sadder aspect. There are
the falling leaves, there is a sense of destruction. If the
spring was the time to plant, then this is the time to pluck
up what is planted, and can also be the time to cast away.
It has been said that this is the season of maturity and of
incipient decay. It is also the time when we return from
our holidays to our work, from the relaxing days to
completing plans we made long ago. Autumn gives a

busy few months, combining rejoicing at the completion of the harvest and sadness that it is all past.

So we come to *winter*, which is all too often parodied as a grim season. We sing about it:

> 'Tis winter now; the fallen snow
>   Has left the heavens all coldly clear;
> Through leafless boughs the sharp winds blow,
>   And all the earth lies dead and drear.[14]

Sometimes we would like to get through it as quickly as possible so that the returning spring may rid us of rheumatic pains and chills. If only we could hibernate! Yet there is so much more to winter than that. These are days when many of us do the things we neglected in summer, hours when there is a greater cosiness about our friendships as we meet in homes which are warmed, whether with fires or central heating, or in churches and social centres. Particularly it is the time when we prepare for Christmas. The glory of the snow causes some to be enthusiastic, though not all share the enthusiasm, and possibly there are more snow-covered days in remembrance than in fact. And with the New Year come the preparations for spring. The garden, the countryside, may look dead but we know that soon life will reveal itself and we plan accordingly.

Which is your favourite season? Possibly spring and summer will have the greater number of supporters but there are those who prefer autumn or even winter. Coventry Patmore wrote:

> I, singularly moved
> To love the lovely that are not beloved,
> Of all the Seasons, most
> Love Winter, and to trace
> The sense of Trophonian pallor on her face.
> It is not death, but plenitude of peace.
>
> Though not a whisper of her voice he hear,
> The buried bulb does know
> The signals of the year
> And hails far Summer with his lifted spear.[15]

13

The wonder of the four seasons is not only in themselves but in the sure knowledge that they will come again. They are a part of the rhythm of life. If at times summer seems unbearably hot, the cool days of autumn will soon be here. If winter seems prolonged spring is always just round the corner. Gordon Manley's words, 'Our seasons in the British Isles are only slightly accentuated, so that all through the year there are days which might belong to any month',[16] are true in a very limited way.

The Week

The *week* also provides its times and seasons. This week of seven days as we know it has a Jewish origin and is a period common also to Mohammedans and Christians. As we think of it we may well see that for us each day has its special significance. So Mrs Hague exemplified. For the majority Monday is the day for returning to work and probably each succeeding day has a special significance. In an office there are jobs to be done each day; if left over, the following days are crowded. Life moves on inexorably until Saturday, often seeming to move far too quickly. Saturday and Sunday have a feeling of holiday about them. Many people find the importance of having a well-divided, well-ordered week, and to most Sunday is still a day which is different from the others. For some of us it is a day of worship when we concentrate upon thoughts of God, when conscience is sharpened and cleansed, and we are free to worship God as conscience directs. We who are nonconformists often rejoice that our forefathers gained this freedom of worship. But it has brought also freedom not to worship, and Sunday is in this country for larger numbers a time when they do the odd jobs around the house, meet with friends, go out into the country or to the seaside, and find it is indeed a day of rest. Some of those who fight to maintain a Sunday when normal industry and commerce are suspended are not always doing so from religious motives. They believe in the value of a time of rest, and the Christian who sometimes makes his

Sunday a time of over-activity should remember that Sunday is a replacement for the Jewish Sabbath which was a day of rest. The writer to the Hebrews emphasises this in talking of the Sabbath. Even God had to rest. 'So then, there remains a sabbath rest for the people of God; for whoever enters God's rest ceases from his labours as God did from his.'[17] The rhythm of life continually includes the opportunity for relaxation, whether it be in the four seasons, in the week or in the day. It is indeed a curse not to be able to rest. Ministers may sometimes live blighted lives because they are too busy. I remember how challenged I was to read some words of John Oman in which he wrote for ministers:

> Greater than work is quietness of spirit. What could we do more for our restless age than give men some taste of it even one day in seven? And how shall we give, if we have not got it? . . . For this quest it is necessary to be, at least in some measure, a man of leisure. This does not mean being without work. It is rather a way of doing our work.[18]

These words apply to us all, to the lay member as well as the minister, the non-Christian as well as the Christian, to the politician, the teacher, the farmer, the housewife, the labourer. We do love to have people think we are busy. We and they need our restfulness.

For some Sunday is too much a day of rest. They do not know what to do with it. The day drags on and they are glad when Monday comes and the rhythm is restored.

The Day

Each *day* has its own natural rhythm. In the morning we awake, willingly or unwillingly. After the opening hour or so, in most cases work makes its demand, and morning and afternoon in this country are the times for labour with a break for lunch. It is possible for some to have a rest after lunch. Do we miss something in not having a siesta? It is wise to keep at least a little time for relaxation, chatting , even dozing. However, people differ in their ways of using the time and often the evening is the time for relaxing, for following one's own interests, for deepening friendships, and in some cases to learn more of our faith and to attend to the business of the church or other organisation that claims our interest. Night is the time for sleep and renewal, and how wonderful it is! 'He gives his beloved sleep,' says the Psalmist; and when sleep deserted him Shakespeare's Henry IV cried out, 'Sleep, O gentle sleep, Nature's soft nurse.' Sleep prepares us for the continuing rhythm of the next day.

This seems perhaps too idyllic. There are those who know little of the rhythm of the day for they have no regular work. Some have retired and cannot establish any kind of rhythm. And while sleep is an essential part of the rhythm, there are those who cannot sleep because of persistent pain, and many rehearse all the cares and problems of the day. They dread the coming day, and the darkness makes everything seem worse. Help may be given but it is not always effective. Sleeping tablets in particular often fail and can easily become habit-forming. When sleep has been difficult I have sometimes recalled:

When in the night I sleepless lie,
My soul with heavenly thoughts supply.[19]

Unfortunately, often my thoughts are far from heavenly yet it has been a time when apart from planning sermons I have recalled some of the causes I · have for thanksgiving. They abound so much that I have fallen asleep before I can hope to remember all. It is good advice to:

Make much of thanksgiving. We may come to an end of confession, many as our sins are. We shall never come to an end of thanksgiving, for God's blessings are the outpourings of infinite, eternal love.[20]

And when the night is past and a new day dawns, the rhythm is there again.

These are the seasons of nature that make up life as we live it. In a sense they cannot change. The four seasons are fixed, the week is a round that we have firmly established, and if not the seven-day week we have there would be another. The day must advance and decline. Nevertheless, the seasons shade into one another, but it is only in a world of fantasy that the distinctions are lost. Titania, in *A Midsummer Night's Dream*, talks of a world where all the seasons become confused:

> The spring, the summer,
> The chiding autumn, angry winter, change
> Their wonted liveries; and the mazed world,
> By their increase, now knows not which is which.

In our world it is not so. True, the weather plays tricks and we describe some days as unseasonable. A cold wind blows in August; there is a warming sunshine in February; but behind all this there is a basic pattern; we can rely on the seasons. It may be that sometimes the demands of work or pleasure turn night into day but the difference is still there. Outwardly also we may see many changes that we have ourselves made in the seasons. At the end of the second world war, on holiday in Suffolk, I joined with others in helping to gather the harvest. Now, not far from that area I sometimes see the farmers at work. The machinery is different, the old sheaves of which we sing in harvest services are no more but the seasons remain.

So we need the special contribution of each season and every day, and they all speak of aspects of our faith. To that I now turn.

Seasons of Faith

Ask now of the days that are past, which were before you, since the day that God created man upon the earth, and ask from one end of heaven to the other, whether such a great thing as this has ever happened or was ever heard of. . . .
To you it was shown, that you might know that the Lord is God; there is no other besides him.

Deuteronomy 4:32, 35

Do not preach the duty of love, but the duty of faith. Do not begin by telling men in God's name that they should love one another. That is no more than an amiable gospel. And it is an impossible gospel till faith gives the power to love. They cannot do it. Tell them God has loved them. . . . Preach faith and the love will grow out of it itself.

P. T. Forsyth

. . . Take your share of suffering for the gospel in the power of God, who saved us and called us with a holy calling, not in virtue of our works but in virtue of his own purpose and the grace which he gave in Christ Jesus ages ago, and now has manifested through the appearing of our Saviour Christ Jesus, who abolished death and brought life and immortality to light through the gospel.
Follow the pattern of the sound words which you have heard from me, in the faith and love which are in Christ Jesus; guard the truth which has been entrusted to you by the Holy Spirit who dwells within us.

2 Timothy 1:8-10; 13, 14

How can we guard our unbelief,
Make it bear fruit to us? — the problem here.
Just when we are safest, there's a sunset touch,
A fancy from a flower-bell, someone's death,
A chorus-ending from Euripides —
And that's enough for fifty hopes and fears
As old and new at once as Nature's self,
To rap and knock and enter in our soul.

Robert Browning, *Bishop Brougham's Apology*

THREE

Seasons of Faith

There is a rhythm in the Christian life as well as nature and in the division of weeks and days. I have already indicated something of this in speaking of the rhythm of the week and the use of Sunday. I now look further at the natural divisions and see how they illuminate the life of faith.

We need the morning and the spring. These are the times when faith begins or is renewed. You are fortunate if you can recall such a period. It may be associated with a particular day or event when God broke into your life. It may have been a more gradual experience. For some today this springlike experience is found in the charismatic movement in various forms, or in the Mission England gatherings. I recall how many of my contemporaries found something of spring and renewal in the Oxford Group Movement (later known as Moral Rearmament). Sometimes this renewal follows what may have seemed to be a winter of faith, or we seem to be in the morning after a night of despair.

> Such clouds of nameless trouble cross
> All night below the darken'd eyes;
> With morning wakes the will, and cries,
> 'Thou shalt not be the fool of loss!'[21]

Or the spring and morning of faith may be something almost unnoticed; we may have grown into it through the loving care of others. But however wonderful be our experience of the dawn of a revived or a new faith we cannot stay there. We have other seasons to discover. In particular we need to beware of despising those seasons which do not have the liveliness of spring.

We need the midday and the summer. After the renewal there come growth and consolidation. There is

19

work to be done and the days may seem long and the weeks, like summer itself, dry and tiring. There will be periods like this in the life of a church. These are the days of testing, these are the days of real growth. They may seem sometimes to have little to thrill or excite us though an imaginative approach will reveal to us their living interest. If the church is to be a true church, if we are to be mature men and women of faith, we need these seasons. It would be a sorry world if there were only spring and no summer.

We need the evening and the autumn. This is the time when the fruits of the past day and the preceding months may be gathered in. It is the season of maturity; we have grown. How different are the gardens and the fields now from what they were six months ago. How much more mature we sometimes feel in the evening than in the morning; we have learned more. Have you ever noticed how continually in his letters Paul stresses the need for growth? In Ephesians we read that the gifts of Christ were 'for the equipment of the saints, for the work of ministry, for building up the body of Christ, until we all attain to the unity of the faith and of the knowledge of the Son of God, to mature manhood, to the measure of the stature of the fulness of Christ'.[22] There is no virtue in remaining in the spring or early summer. I am not greatly impressed when someone tells me that he has the same simple faith that he had forty years ago when a boy. Faith should have developed with life's experiences. It should have matured through learning more about God in Christ. A ninety-year-old former student of Cheshunt College used to send the Library small collections of verse he had written. *Fruit from an Old Tree* was followed by *More Fruit from an Old Tree* and then by *Yet More Fruit from an Old Tree.* Ninety years old and still growing! When that attitude is found there is peace in the evening as in autumn, with a feeling of fulfilment. It is not discovered by all but we should look for it.

We need the night and the winter. In the rhythm of life these are not the end; they lead to morning and spring. They may be seen as a season of rest and of preparation for a new day. This is akin to the rest Jesus promised when he said,

'Come to me, all who labour and are heavy laden, and I will give you rest. Take my yoke upon you, and learn of me; for I am gentle and lowly in heart, and you will find rest for your souls.'[23]

The word 'rest' is not just a lazy contentment. It is the rest which comes from a temporary cessation of labour, or a pause that we may continue. Winter may sometimes be thought of as a period of inactivity but in fact those weeks may also be among the busiest. In church life much of our best work is done here. If it were always summer it is doubtful if there would be much teaching and growing in the faith. And without the night of sleep we shall be unable to face the demands of the next day.

Sometimes night and winter speak to us of the end of this life when the rhythm is completed. But to the Christian that cannot be fully true. The winter, which is as death to many, leads on to a new spring, different from all others. The night passes, the morning breaks. We enter a different, unknown world. From one side we call it death; seen from the side of faith it leads to life and to a new rhythm.

The Christian Calendar

The seasons of the Christian Year provide a more obvious rhythm of faith. I have been looking, with the interest of one not accustomed to regularly using it, at the Alternative Service Book of the Church of England. It begins with the Calendar. First it sets out the Seasons, and every Sunday of the year with the special days is covered. There follow a list of Principal Holy Days, Festivals and Greater Holy Days and Lesser Festivals and Commemorations, Special Days of Prayer and Thanksgiving and Days of Discipline and Self-denial. The year is indeed covered, sometimes it may seem, all too fully. When I was minister of a church and found that to the Church Calendar were added all kinds of special days, with appeals for this and that good cause, I longed for a

21

few Sundays when I could simply declare the Word of God and give some regular teaching. But there is great value in the Calendar and I would never wish to neglect it. It establishes for our faith the rhythm of the Christian life. It began to be observed early in the Christian story. Easter and Pentecost were related to Jewish festivals and, like the Jewish Passover, dates were movable in relation to the moon. In the sixth century, in Rome, the Christian seasons began with the Incarnation, the date being then fixed as 25th March AD 1, which was the supposed date of the Annunciation, similar to our New Year's Day. As the years went by saints days were added to the cycle of dates which were basic, until we have the Calendar of today.[24]

This basic Calendar now begins with *Advent*, the season leading up to Christmas. In Western Christianity there are four Sundays in Advent. We use it as a time of preparation for Christmas so that we are led gradually into the wonder of the incarnation. There is also an important second emphasis in Advent. It is not only the time for remembering the coming of Christ 2,000 years ago but also his second coming as Judge at the last days. Thus past and future are brought together. However we interpret the meaning of the second coming we see that the Lord of the present and the future, as of the past, is the same Jesus Christ for whose coming we prepare in Advent. The days leading to Christmas become a source of joy and solemnity.

Advent culminates in *Christmas*. The story of the development into the kind of Christmas we know in our own country is an interesting one. Our Christmas was not a feature of early Christianity. The first reference to the date of 25th December was in AD 336 and this date was probably chosen to replace the Roman celebration of Saturnalia and other pagan festivals. We may ignore the many debates about the actual date of the birth of Jesus for nobody knows for certain which it was. It is the developments within the 19th century that have made the Christmas we know today, that of the Christmas tree, the parties, the rejoicing and the giving and receiving of presents, and the gigantic sending of cards. The introduction of the Christmas tree by the Prince Consort and the novels of Charles Dickens helped to make Christmas a central theme in the Christian year, and many people echo the words of Charles Dickens:

> I have always thought of Christmas time, when it has come round—apart from the veneration due to its sacred name and origin, if anything belonging to it can be apart from that—as a good time; a kind, forgiving, charitable, pleasant time: the only time I know of, in the long calendar of the year, when men and women seem by one consent to open their shut-up hearts freely, and to think of people below them as if they really were fellow-passengers to the grave, and not another race of creatures bound on other journeys. And therefore, though it has never put a scrap of gold or silver in my pocket, I believe that it *has* done me good, and *will* do me good: and I say, God bless it![25]

We would wish to express some of his thoughts differently but this is the Christmas we know and we sometimes regret that what Dickens saw as inseparable is often divided, as when shops try to sell 'Religious Christmas cards', as though there really could be a true Christmas without the religious content. We may rather rejoice that in the Calendar of the year many who do not normally attend church will come to worship at Christmas because deep down they feel the importance of the season. Can we build on that?

Closely related to Christmas is *Epiphany*, celebrated on 6th January. It originated in the Eastern Church in the third century when the baptism of Jesus was celebrated, and along with Easter and Pentecost it was at that time regarded as one of the three great festivals of the Church. In the West the association was more with the manifestation of Christ to the Gentiles, as seen in the coming of the Magi, the wise men from the East. While in many churches there is little to distinguish this from Christmas and we read the story of the wise men along with that of the shepherds in our Christmas services, it is

23

well to keep in mind that from the beginning Christ is to be seen as Lord of all peoples, born not only for the Jews but for the Gentiles as well.

All too soon after the Christmas rejoicing at the birth of Jesus comes the season of *Lent*, covering the forty days before Easter. In the first three centuries of the life of the Church there were normally only three days for the preparation for Easter. Customs varied in different churches but there was a common emphasis on the need to fast, and the forty days were linked with the forty-day fasts of Moses and Elijah, but more frequently with Jesus' own fasting.[26] Lent became increasingly a time of penance, discipline, and in more recent years a time for almsgiving, and a giving of more time than usual to religious exercises. In churches in our own country more emphasis is being laid on the following of Jesus in his ministry from the time of the temptations on to Calvary, with a study of the faith, series of sermons and evening house groups, often of an ecumenical nature. The element of fasting is not so predominant, though still many feel uneasy about this, and some 'give up' smoking, sugar or other luxuries during Lent, sometimes rushing eagerly to restore them at Easter. So the season means more than once it did but I wonder if we have yet worked out its meaning for our churches and ourselves.

Lent comes to its fulfilment in *Passiontide* and *Holy Week*. The final days of Jesus' life on earth are commemorated. All parts of the Christian Church observe the week and the rites go back to the fourth century. Each in our own way, in private Bible reading and prayer, in groups and in worship services, we recall and seek the meaning of the suffering of Jesus, and every day is rich in remembrance. We may not feel that we are able to explain fully all that we mean by the cross of Jesus, but we glimpse its importance for mankind and for us individually. A few make pilgrimages to sacred places, if possible to Jerusalem itself, and we all contemplate the cross. *Good Friday* sums up the whole life of Christ. We know that he died for us. Here is a mystery that

24

theologians and poets have tried to express but always do so incompletely.

> And was there then no other way
> For God to take? I cannot say;
> I only thank him day by day
> Who saved me through my Saviour.[27]

There is a pause after Good Friday. Saturday was a day of waiting, as it still is for us. We have sorrow of heart because Christ has died, but since we know what happened afterwards there is satisfying expectancy. So *Easter* comes, the greatest of all seasons of the Christian year, that which is central to our faith. It is also the oldest celebration of the Calendar. In the Early Church catechumens prayed all Saturday night and were baptised on Easter morning, dying to the old life and rising to the new. Later, churches and whole cities were illuminated to welcome Easter morning. The feeling that after tragedy comes triumph overwhelms the Christian, and in countries like our own the link with spring makes even clearer the newness of life in Christ. God raised him from the dead. Even a cursory reading of Acts and the Epistles brings out this assurance that the Christ who was raised from the dead dies no more.[28] Easter is a continuing experience.

The season of Easter assurance was followed by a period of uncertainty, not so much about the Resurrection but about what the followers of Jesus should be doing. They chose someone to take over Judas Iscariot's place, they met for fellowship and prayer. Then came the vivid experience of the coming of the Holy Spirit at *Pentecost.* Originating in the Jewish Feast of Weeks, which fell on the fiftieth day after Passover, it quickly became a feast day of the Christian Church. The period between Easter and Pentecost was a time of rejoicing as well as waiting. Today there is among Christians an increasing emphasis laid on the meaning of Pentecost, Whit Sunday, and this may be helped by the separation of the spring bank holiday and Whit Monday, so that they do not always fall on the same day. To some it is second only to Easter with the stress on the power of the Holy Spirit as being available still. Yet often there is a touch of nostalgia and regret. This happened once; if only it could happen again! I recall the words of a Negro Salvationist as he watched by the tomb of William Booth and thought of the spirit-filled life of his hero, 'Do it again, Lord. Do it again.' In fact he has done it again and many are the victories of the Spirit today, some of them obvious to all, and accompanied by great excitement, while other victories are seen as a quiet influence resting in a humble heart.[29] Even as Christ dies no more, so the Holy Spirit continues to be given and often in surprising ways.

There is a further season, *Trinity Sunday*. This was not observed as a day of remembrance of the Trinity until the Middle Ages. It is less frequently celebrated, especially in our Free Churches, mainly I suspect because we do not understand the Trinity. The fact is that it brings together all the seasons of the Calendar. It reveals the greatness of God, made known to us as the Creator of all, the God who came in Christ to live our life and to die for us, and who has ever been at work in the Holy Spirit. He is the God seen in himself to be personal and therefore able to make contact with us and we with him. Do not neglect Trinity Sunday.

There follow the long unmarked weeks, formerly denoted as 'after Trinity' and now more frequently described as 'after Pentecost'. There are twenty-three Sundays in all. To me they are times when we can work out what the Gospel means for us. Harold K. Moulton has expressed it well in introducing a chapter on *Christian Conduct*:

The main events of the Christian Year are crowded into its first six months. We celebrate in succession Christ's birth, death, resurrection, ascension and the coming of the Spirit, all of which stimulate our thoughts and wills as they were intended to do. Then we settle down to a more humdrum period. It is impossible to get wildly enthusiastic about, say, the twenty-second Sunday after Trinity.

But this is the period in which our reaction to the great Christian events is put to the test. Believing in the work of Christ, are we going to live according to what he has given us? The Church of South India has wisely emphasised this by speaking not of Sundays after Trinity, but of Sundays after Pentecost, the time when we prove the gift of the Holy Spirit.[30]

As we go through these seasons of the Christian year many questions arise: When was Jesus born? What do we understand by the Virgin Birth? How does the Crucifixion affect our lives? What was the nature of the Resurrection? What really happened at Pentecost? To try to give the briefest of answers would require another volume, and many are the books that have been written to help us. My concern is to bring home the range of the Christian Calendar and the fact that we need to celebrate all the seasons. If we do not follow the Calendar we may well neglect central aspects of the Christian faith. However important are the celebratory seasons of the Church we do not keep to them alone. The content of public worship should be tested by the Calendar. We do not keep the remembrance of the Incarnation only at Christmas, and Dr Dale was right when he called the Carrs Lane congregation to sing an Easter hymn every Sunday morning, since he knew that all worship is a celebration of the Resurrection. The glory of the cross of Christ, the thanksgiving for the Holy Spirit, the wonder at creation and at the coming of the child Jesus, need to be with us every day. We will never tire of that repetition.

Worship and Prayer

There are many other seasons important for our Christian faith and living. We need times of worship and prayer, and to some extent we create these for ourselves. They cannot be separated though often we speak as though worship is what we do with others, especially in public worship on Sundays, while prayer is what we do on our own, often privately. But the two influence each other and we pray as we worship and worship while we pray.

The quality of our public worship will be impoverished if we do not give time to private prayer, and the prayers we offer in home or in the streets or at work are often shaped by the content of public worship. For a recent study of worship, see Bernard Thorogood's volume in this series, *Our Father's House, An Approach to Worship.*

Doubt and Faith

Other seasons come upon us in our Christian life. There are times of doubt and of assured faith. Sometimes they really do seem to be seasonal and we should all beware of criticising people who feel differently. Some of those who have a deep certainty about their faith, who often boast that they never have doubts, look scornfully, pityingly, on others who confess to doubts, almost suggesting that something is morally wrong with them. And many a doubter says that belief comes too easily to the people of the assured faith, as though they had not even asked questions. Men and women of faith are accused of having closed minds. But here as elsewhere we are all amazingly' different and so many factors, such as health, experiences of disappointment or success, may influence us. The very seasons of the year, the day of the week, the time of the day, may help us to believe or add to our unbelief.

You may recall that the beauty of a spring morning, coming just after Easter, made you want to sing with Pippa 'God's in his heaven—All's right with the world'.[31] On a dull December evening, when you recounted to yourself all the evils of life, probably nothing seemed right. This is not to suggest that faith and doubt are entirely governed by outward circumstance. Faith may well be the result of a continuing reflection on life and on all that God has done, as seen in the seasons we have reviewed. Doubt may also follow from our thinking and reading about life and its mysteries and miseries. We cannot lightly dismiss the Ethiopian famine or the violence in the inner cities of Britain. 'My hosanna', says Dostoevsky, 'has passed through great whirlwinds of doubt.' Neither can we be content with the seasons of doubt, and certainly there is no virtue in boasting about

28

it. I recall that Dr Sydney Cave, Principal of New College, London, was reticent about the treatment of faith and doubt in Tennyson's *In Memoriam*, for he could not go along with:

> There lives more faith in honest doubt,
> Believe me, than in half the creeds.

With Dr Cave's hesitation I would agree; yet I find something true in the words following:

> He fought his doubts and gather'd strength,
> He would not make his judgment blind,
> He faced the spectres of the mind
> And laid them: thus he came at length
> To find a stronger faith his own.[32]

The season of faith may well follow the time of doubt. So much depends upon our willingness to face both honestly.

Seasons That Come Not Again

All the world's a stage,
And all the men and women merely players:
They have their exits and their entrances;
And one man in his time plays many parts,
His act being seven ages. At first the infant,
Mewling and puking in the nurse's arms.
And then the whining schoolboy, with his satchel
And shining morning face, creeping like a snail
Unwillingly to school. And then the lover,
Sighing like furnace, with a woeful ballad
Made to his mistress' eyebrow. Then a soldier,
Full of strange oaths, and bearded like the pard,
Zealous in honour, sudden and quick in quarrel,
Seeking the bubble reputation
Even in the cannon's mouth. And then the justice,
In fair round belly with good capon lin'd,
With eyes severe, and beard of formal cut,
Full of wise saws and modern instances;
And so he plays his part. The sixth age shifts
Into the lean and slipper'd pantaloon,
With spectacles on nose and pouch on side,
His youthful hose well sav'd a world too wide
For his shrunk shank; and his big manly voice,
Turning again towards childish treble, pipes
And whistles in his sound. Last scene of all,
That ends this strange eventful history,
Is second childishness, and mere oblivion,
Sans teeth, sans eyes, sans taste, sans everything.

William Shakespeare, *As You Like It*

I have come to feel that there is hardly anything more radically mean and deteriorating than, as it were, *sulking through the inevitable*, and simply counting the hours till it passes.

Baron von Hügel

Though by this time you ought to be teachers, you need someone to teach you the ABC of God's oracles over again; it has come to this, that you need milk instead of solid food. Anyone who lives on milk, being an infant, does not know what is right. But grown men can take solid food; their perceptions are trained by long use to discriminate between good and evil.

Hebrews 5:12-14, *NEB*

FOUR

Seasons That Come Not Again

So far I have chiefly been concerned with seasons that come and go. There will be another day, a further spring. Christmas may come but once a year but it will come again next year; indeed we are already counting the shopping days to it. Some seasons however come but once and cannot be repeated. Ecclesiastes' first seasons were 'a time to be born, and a time to die'. We must accept each season as it comes. This is obviouly true of the different ages of life. Our world is not the same as Shakespeare's, yet our lives also are divided into separate seasons that will never come again.

Before I speak of the main unrepeatable seasons, however, I want to make clear that we must not take these seasons so seriously that we deny man's ability to adapt to them. We may speak, for example, of a time to learn at school or university, and we are rightly told that we must use the times well since there will never be that opportunity again. It is good advice but fortunately it is also true that some people make up for their lost opportunities. We have grown accustomed to the fact that many who did not take full advantage of the opportunities at school or university, or who did not have such opportunities, have found a new world of study in the Open University. There have been those who seemed slow to develop who have found challenges in business or in war that caused them to know the joy of discovery and achievement in later life. This late development is true of the Christian life. There is a character in the New Testament, often underrated and confused with another of the same name—James. The one I speak of was James, the brother of our Lord. In later years he was acclaimed by those who knew him to be a good, a righteous man. Here is a description from a second-century writer:

> James, the brother of our Lord, succeeded to the government of the Church in conjunction with the apostles. . . . He was holy from his mother's womb; and he drank no wine nor strong drink, nor did he eat flesh. . . . He was in the habit of entering alone into the temple, and was frequently found upon his knees begging forgiveness for the people, so that his knees became hard like those of a camel, in consequence of constantly bending them in his worship of God.[33]

Not exactly our idea of piety today but the interesting fact is that he had been a late developer. During the lifetime of Jesus, his brother, there had been no sign that James understood him or wished to follow him. He was among the brethren who did not believe in Jesus. He had seen how Jesus cared for the family after the death of Joseph, their father, he must have sensed the wonder of Jesus' own life but in spite of this relationship he could not accept Jesus for what he was. It was only on the other side of the Resurrection that he came to believe in Jesus and was accepted as the leader of the church in Jerusalem. I find him a most encouraging character, for he overcame the lost opportunities.[34]

On a larger scale however we cannot have again what once happened. Childhood may be extended, maturity be slow in coming, and there are old people who are said to have found the secret of perpetual youth, but the seasons of age cannot really be repeated and to live with any joy and success this must be accepted. As a twentieth-century poet put it:

> Last year's words belong to last year's language
> And next year's words await another voice.[35]

We can, of course, recall past seasons in gratitude or relief, and sometimes with regret, in the spirit of Augustine who wrote in his *Confessions*, 'Allow me, I beseech you, to trace again in memory my past deviations and to offer you a sacrifice of joy.'[36] But memory is never sufficient and cannot take us back to the past so that it becomes the present to be enjoyed as once it was. Our responsibility is to live now, to relate to the seasons of life where we are. So let us go through these seasons.

Our Four Ages

There is the season of *Childhood*. It is easy to idealise this and there was the grimmer side in the last century when children were often exploited. The view that children were small adults or that childhood passed very quickly may be traced back to the Spartan boys who were early taken from their families to be trained as warriors. The treatment of children in an earlier industrial age, when they were expected to be wage-earners when far too young, was exposed in the novels of Charles Dickens and in the poem of Elizabeth Barrett Browning, *The Cry of the Children*. Childhood is meant to be enjoyed, and in the treatment of children this century this has been stressed. The study of the children, with their gifts, their needs, their abilities, has been basic to education. They are not simply young adults. Of childhood and of youth this needs to be emphasised. There is something for them to enjoy and something for them to contribute. I saw once a cartoon which showed a young person surrounded by all his interests, home, school, youth club, as well as his dreams. It was called *My Job, My Future* and the boy was saying:

> Oh, joy it is to be alive in such a dawn as this,
> When youth is king, and adult slaves prepare my future bliss;
> Where'er I turn, a helping hand is stretched to offer joy;
> But how I wish they'd leave me time to learn to be a boy.

There follows the season of *Youth*. There seems to be little agreement when childhood passes into youth and youth ends. I recall many a debate about the fixing of the age. Younger people themselves do not know what are the limits. At a youth conference years ago, when speaking of the over-twenty-fives, one young man said, 'They've had their day.' So quickly youth passes! Today the tendency is to place the move from childhood to youth earlier so that youth clubs include those who a short time ago would have been called children. However we limit youth it is a time of mixed preparation and fulfilment, of insight, hope and achievement. For many it is a painful period, with self-consciousness, fears and uncertainties about the present and the future. It has been made more difficult in recent years by the lack of jobs and the fear that gradually increases that the young have no assured future. In spite of this, youth has a contribution of its own to make as we have seen in the United Reformed Church. It presents a challenge to a world that is often tired. At best young people are anxious to serve rather than to be served. Their interests may change but in essence they have the same characteristics as their predecessors.

The season of *Maturity* leads into busy days. Youth is past. Some find that difficult to accept and they try to hang on to the past. There are few more pathetic sights than to see someone clinging whether in dress, ideas or interests to a youth that is over. There will always be some overspill and we thank God for those who in later years retain the zest and liveliness they had when young, but they must also have the marks of maturity. The young themselves despise the hangers-on to their youth who think that they can influence a new generation by behaving like them. Young people want the interest and the sympathy of their seniors but not the imitation. I have often noticed that among the best youth leaders are those who are a few years removed from the young, and there are old people who have a wonderful understanding of the young. The years of maturity may be long, with increasing responsibility, and often they are wearying, frustrating and disappointing. Yet they have their own rewards and are for many a time of deepening understanding and experience, of hope as well as fulfilment, of parenthood and of special opportunities. As we look back we may see that it was in these years that we discovered some of the best things life has given us. Much of what I have said is summed up in some words of

the Victorian preacher F. W. Robertson, though in part
he overstates his case:

> To a man of middle life existence is no longer a dream
> but a reality. He has not much more new to look for-
> ward to, for the character of his life is generally fixed
> by that time. His profession, his home, his occupations,
> will be for the most part what they are now. He will
> make few new acquaintances—no new friends. . . .
> When the first grey hairs become visible—when the
> unwelcome truth fastens itself upon the mind that a
> man is no longer going up the hill, but down, and that
> the sun is already westering, he looks back on things
> behind. Now this is a natural feeling, but is it the high
> Christian tone of feeling? . . . We may assuredly an-
> swer, No. We who have an inheritance incorruptible
> and undefiled, and that fadeth not away, what have we
> to do with things past? When we were children we
> thought as children. But now there lies before us
> manhood, with its earnest work.[37]

The social changes since Robertson's day have also
meant changes for the middle-aged. They move from
place to place more than they did. Often they make new
friendships in the summer years, and old age seems far
away when they are so busy. The true picture for
maturity is that when there lie before us manhood and
womanhood, with their earnest work.

So we come to *Old Age*, in itself a lengthening period
for most people nowadays. Life is prolonged through
improving health services and a higher standard of living.
So, when do you become old? I have known wise old men
and women in their twenties and youthful eighty-year-
olds. At one time they were regarded as old at sixty, and
then at seventy (with the support of the psalmist),[38]
though to children forty is old age. When I was fifty I
remarked at a conference that I was getting old and next
day received a card from some young people present
which read, 'Don't worry about getting old. You've got.'
It is good if we are able not to worry, perhaps to be able to
say with Mrs Pearsall Smith:

'We are in 1903 and I am nearly seventy-one years old. I always thought I should love to grow old, and I find it even more delightful than I thought. . . . So you may think of me as happy and contented, surrounded with unnumbered blessings, and delighted to be seventy-one years old.'[39]

But not all can say that. For some old age is a time of weakness, anxiety and fear. Long years of uselessness await them. It is particularly hard for those who once were in positions of leadership and who cannot adjust, while for others there is loneliness made worse by ill-health. Old age is so severe for some that there are those who advocate euthanasia. When they think of the growing number of helpless older people they suggest that a painless death would be a way of dealing with the non-earning elderly population. We can understand also the feeling of those who are in continual pain and who are tempted to long for death. Yet can we really favour this as a policy? The deep-seated conviction that our lives are not our own to dispose, the fact that most hesitate at the brink, the danger of any policy of euthanasia getting into the wrong hands, make us pause. Those of us who enjoy good health might hesitate to say that such a view is never right but there is also another side to the question, as any minister who has spent time visiting the elderly knows. Many who have suffered strokes or who have incurable (often painful) ailments show a serenity and a love of life that shames our complainings. Often it is their Christian faith which carries them positively through the changing years. Leslie Tizard once wrote:

The art of growing old depends, more than on anything else, upon having a religion which deepens and develops with every stage of life. . . . God is so big that if we know him aright he can satisfy us at every stage of life. The Christ who met our needs at twenty is not adequate at forty, when we have to face problems we could not even glimpse at half that age.[40]

There are sadly old people who can no longer go forth to the fight but there are also those like a man of eighty-three of whom it was said he was 'like an ancient olive, with a mere shell for its trunk, yet indomitably throwing new shoots on top—green against the grey'. Old age is not mainly a time of regret that the joys of earlier achievement are passed but may be a time of continued reflection, even of further activity. It is no more the time for staying in the chimney corner.[41]

Work and Retirement

Another way of looking at the fixed seasons of life is to see them as periods of *growing up, working* and *retirement.* Of *growing up* I say little here. It is a longer period than formerly, yet always it looks forward as well as enjoying the present.

The season of *work* may be a long season, fifty years or more, though with prolonged education and earlier retirement, it is becoming a shorter period. Happy the man or woman to whom work comes as a vocation, who enjoys what is being done day by day and feels that it is worth while. It does not take away the dull and monotonous tasks but sets them into a purpose. For many, work is the one means of earning money. They don't really enjoy it. It is the evenings, the weekend, the holidays that provide the life they desire. For others today there is no paid work. The horrors of poverty in its extreme form that earlier accompanied unemployment have largely passed but the feeling of uselessness remains. There is no easy solution to the problem though each political party presents its claim to cure. It is a bigger problem than we wish to admit and it may be that we shall only find a solution when we separate the actual earning of income from the wherewithal we need, so that there will be shorter hours of work for most and more leisure. This has already partly come about. It then means that we face a season of work which includes leisure, and that our education must be directed towards this truer preparation for life. However we see it, one of the seasons for us all will be the prolonged season when we work officially or unofficially.

Yet however we regard the main years of life, they lead

to *retirement*, the time when we cease to earn our living as we would once have put it. In the early 19th century there were a few people who retired early, even before forty. They were the wealthy who often gave themselves then to charitable works. How much the missionary societies owed to people like them. The vast majority had to labour on and when retirement came there might be no money to keep them; they had to rely on relatives or the local authority which often meant the Poor House. It is different now. Most have retired by sixty-five and increasingly early retirement is sought and supported. I am not competent to write on the economic problems this brings for businesses and for the nation as a whole. It is a serious issue for government. What I seek to do is to share some comments about retirement. I retired later than most and have now been retired for seven years. The days have been busy and I do not feel that I have yet worked out a philosophy of retirement, and in any case it differs so widely for different people. When I retired I was given a book about retirement. Most of it was unread and passed to a jumble sale. However, over the years some things become increasingly clear.

Retirement must in part be what the word suggests. We break from the usual way of living and working. Many find that hard. For those whose work is home-based there is a value in moving from where you have been living. Those who daily went elsewhere to work may find this of less importance. Yet the moving away has its dangers and the pundits often say that it is unwise to move from the familiar. In some cases that is so but here I see one of the incidental values of the Church. As members of a church we know that wherever we go we are likely to meet Christian friends. The Church is ready to welcome us. Or is it always so? I wonder sometimes how readily some churches receive strangers. The welcoming of newcomers, particularly of the old, is one of our most important pastoral opportunities.

Though retirement is a turning away from the days when we worked hard to earn our living it is still often a very busy time. It should not be so busy that we proudly say to enquirers, 'I am busier than when I worked.' That does not say much for the work we once did. There may be some justification for saying, 'I don't know how I found time for work.' Yet the enjoyment of relaxation as well as activity should be ours at such a time. We have time for our friends and opportunities to spend more quiet days and evenings. Sometimes in the morning we may suddenly decide to go into the country or city. We are controllers of our time more than we used to be.

Retirement also means for many the opportunity to explore new fields. In some cases this means doing something that is quite different and it has all the thrill of new discovery. Look at the army of ageing artists who travel around the country and often abroad, showing skills they never knew they possessed. Recall the many who practise crafts for the first time or go back to interests they left long ago. Some garden more, often having too large a garden to care for. There are always jobs about the house which they were too busy to do before and new skills may be developed. Those who have a taste for study may tackle new subjects. A learned theologian told me once that he seldom read theology in retirement; he had turned to history. Others move from the subjects they mastered, perhaps taught, to travel and biography, to novels and even philosophy. There are often opportunities to travel and daily walking brings both health and refreshment. Yet time need not be spent only with those of similar age. There are organisations and interests that bring in meetings with people of different ages. In the church there is a worship that may well be for a variety of ages and meetings to cover differing needs. Perhaps especially for some who have been over-busy there is the opportunity to think and to pray, and in a sense to prepare for the unknown future.

Some will be unwilling to accept retirement. They are probably in a position to continue what they were doing or to do in part what once was their work. It is easy to hang on too long. By so doing we may get in other people's way, denying them opportunities we once had, discouraging them from bringing their own contribution, while we ourselves are delaying too long our acceptance of retirement.

Happy are those who have the resources to embark on new adventures in retirement, to make intriguing articles of beauty, to read new books. Not all can do this for some have lost the physical control necessary. Here is the opportunity for people of all ages to help. The social services do a wonderful job for many of them but they need more aid. Here is a great field of service open to the community and to the churches.

And there are Other Seasons

There are so many ways of looking at the seasons of life and faith. There are the periods when we learn a great deal, and not only at school. There are times of achievement and these may come unexpectedly. There are other times when nothing seems to happen, hours when there is little that is creative. There are the seasons when we make friends, often in the early days, and these friendships may remain. There are also times when we lose our friends. One friend in her mid-eighties warned me against growing old, since friends then drop off one by one. But in these days of more frequent changes new friendships may be made when we are old. What were once thought of as being unrepeatable experiences may in fact come again though somewhat differently. This is true of falling in love. The wildness and the joy of that first experience may never be known again but there are times when one partner dies, and at present marriages are often ended in divorce. In neither case is it necessarily taken for granted that there will be no further marriage. I have known many to whom there had been given the experience of a second love. It may not be the same as the first in many respects but it is a joyful fact.

Some of the other seasons remain to be studied but I quote now from Hunter Davies' refreshing biography of William Wordsworth, when he draws attention to the changes in Wordsworth's life and warns against too easily seeing differences in the seasons of life:

40

It is always tempting, though dangerous, to see what others never saw at the time, to stand back with the benefit of hindsight, presuming to detect patterns, pinpointing changes, encapsulating the strands of other people's lives. Yet one can't always rely on the participants to do it for us, since they are rarely aware themselves that they are changing.

William Wordsworth as a young man was different from William Wordsworth as a middle-aged man. Few people would argue about that. When and how and why the changes came about are much more difficult to agree upon, but it seems to me that in about 1805 he reached a watershed in his life. William at thirty-five held rather different views from William at twenty-five though he himself never seems to have remarked on it, which is strange, considering the degree of introspection with which he analysed his poetic development. His close family, his domestic partners, don't seem to have remarked on it either—but then, when you are close to someone, it's hard to see the changes. . . .

One of the dangers in seeing watersheds, and attempting to define changes in someone's personality, is to forget that the young man is still inside the middle-aged body, if rather deeper down, hiding away. William might on the surface have become more reactionary and conservative in these middle years, but he was still liable to surprise.[42]

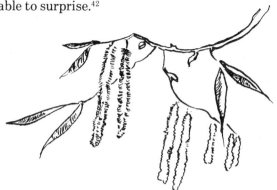

Giving and Receiving

I came that they may have life, and have it abundantly.

The words of Jesus, John 10:10

The King will say . . . 'I was hungry and you gave me food, I was thirsty and you gave me drink, I was a stranger and you welcomed me, I was naked and you clothed me, I was sick and you visited me, I was in prison and you came to me.' Then the righteous will answer him, 'Lord, when did we see thee hungry and feed thee, or thirsty and gave thee drink? And when did we see thee a stranger and welcome thee, or naked and clothe thee? And when did we see thee sick or in prison and visit thee?' And the King will answer them, 'Truly, I say to you, as you did it to one of the least of these my brethren, you did it to me.'

Matthew 25:34-40

When any master holds
'Twixt chin and hand a violin of mine,
He will be glad that Stradivari lived,
Made violins, and made them of the best . . .
I say not God himself can make man's best
Without best men to help him. . . .
'Tis God gives skill,
But not without men's hands: he could not make
Antonio Stradivari's violins
Without Antonio.

George Eliot in *Stradivarius*

If you have doubts about the existence of God or misgivings as to the kind of God he is, I do not think your need will be met by argument. It will be met only by an act of trust on your part. *You must be willing to be found by the pursuing love of God* which will not let you go; to face the challenge which is relentless; to move out fearlessly from your narrow self-centred life into a new, wide, spacious life with Christ at the centre—trusting not in yourself but in the all-sufficient love and power of God.

From a sermon by Leslie J. Tizard
in *Facing Life and Death*

FIVE

Giving and Receiving

When Ecclesiastes wrote of 'a time to plant, and a time to pluck up what is planted' he was speaking to an agricultural community. In the spring the farmer gives to the soil and continues to give. In the harvest, when he plucks up, he receives more than he gave. There are always seasons of giving and receiving. According to the Acts of the Apostles, Paul told the elders of the church at Ephesus that Jesus had said, 'It is more blessed to give than to receive.'[43] You will not find this among the sayings of Jesus recorded in the Gospels. That should not surprise us for Jesus must have said many things that are not recorded by the evangelists. Writers and preachers have often speculated on the reason for the exclusion from the Gospels. Why, for example, did not Luke include the words in his Gospel since he obviously knew them? Such speculation leads nowhere, but one thing is clear. Jesus may well on occasion have used these words but the Gospel is not primarily a call on the disciples to give. They are great recipients. The Gospel, the good news, is first of all what God has done for us in Christ. Paul in his letters emphasises what he had received and how the Christians had received so much from Christ, summing it up in his words to the Corinthians, 'What have you that you did not receive?'[44]

The Young Receive

There are times in life when we need to emphasise receiving. The obvious season of receiving that may be prolonged is that of *childhood.* The care of parents and friends, the growing help of the State, the provision of schools, all recognise that at this stage the child needs a great deal to be given to him. Sometimes the help is organised, as in State benefits, medical care, and schools. At other times it springs from the real basis of all giving and receiving, the love that we have for the child. Is this not a part of the meaning of Infant Baptism? God loves the child before the child loves God. The Church surrounds the child with care and concern before the child can respond. It is a measure of our inadequacy as churches and our failure ourselves to give and to receive that often we do not take this aspect of baptism seriously and fail to follow it through by our help to parents and children. For several years these children will be receiving from the church in worship and in Christian education.

So all through childhood there is much to be received and, more particularly, when life does not go well. Helen Keller, the amazing blind and deaf girl, describes this beautifully in the story of her life:

> Those happy days did not last long. One brief spring, musical with the song of robin and mocking-bird, one summer rich in fruit and roses, one autumn of gold and crimson sped by and left their gifts at the feet of an eager, delighted child. Then, in the dreary month of February, came the illness which closed my eyes and ears and plunged me into the unconsciousness of a new-born baby. . . . The doctor thought I could not live. Early one morning, however, the fever left me as suddenly and mysteriously as it had come. There was great rejoicing in the family, but no one, not even the doctor, knew that I should never see or hear again.

Helen, who had received so much as a small child and now had lost so much, tells how she received in her teacher great gifts:

> Gradually I got used to the silence and darkness that surrounded me and forgot that it had ever been different, until she came—my teacher—who was to set my spirit free.[45]

We can easily recount other stories of the ways in which the young receive, in love, in guidance, in teaching.

The Old Receive

A second season when the emphasis tends to be on

receiving is for the old. For many this is dificult, even poignant. All through history and in different ways in varying civilisations and countries the older have depended upon the family for support. In the West more and more help is given by the State. Some old people find this very hard to accept and here is the poignancy. We all realise that independence of spirit can be good or bad. None of us can be completely independent. Even when senior citizens have sufficient money and good homes and wide interests as I have already suggested, the time comes when they must rely more and more on physical help and that is sometimes rejected or received only with complaint. To be able to receive graciously is often difficult.

The final chapter of John's Gospel is full of deep spiritual insight and human wisdom. Jesus looked lovingly on Peter, independent but never entirely so, strong but with inner weaknesses. How would he face times of restriction when he would be a recipient as well as a giver? 'Truly, truly, I say unto you, when you were young, you girded yourself and walked where you would; but when you are old, you will stretch out your hands, and another will gird you and carry you where you do not wish to go.'[46] The writer saw this as relating to Peter's death but it is also used of the lengthening years. When we come again to a season of receiving we need to cultivate the grace of acceptance.

When we Give

There are seasons when the emphasis is more on what we can give. As the young grow older they rightly believe they have much to offer though sometimes they have their misgivings. When they pass to mature years it is expected that they will make their contribution to the family, to society, to the world, to their church. How wonderfully some achieve this. Look at the memorial stones in churches or graveyards. Maybe you will wonder at the great record of near perfect characters and the story of their constant giving to others. It is not only written of those who died after long lives but some who died young are said to have given abundantly. I have sometimes wondered if the people who died have been over-praised and their blemishes blotted out but we cannot get away from the fact that there are men and women who throughout their lives give generously as they are able, and behind the memorials are millions of people who have no memorial but who accepted and rejoiced in the season of giving. When we think of their lives we realise the truth of the words of Jesus as remembered by Paul.

The dangers of emphasising too much the importance of being givers are many. It may lead to pride. 'We don't depend upon other people; we give more than we receive' is often our attitude. We think of ourselves as the people of strength and wisdom. The world would be a poorer place without us. Maybe it would but we are not the people who should say so. We all know the objectionable aspect of people who are bent upon improving us. They are benefactors in their own eyes and pride overwhelms.

Giving and Receiving

Too great a stress on ourselves as givers also means that we overlook the glorious mixture of life. I am writing of seasons of giving and receiving and, as with many other seasons, they often overlap and interpenetrate. The child is receiving all the time but how much she will give as well as receive! It is not only the pleasure we find in children though that is there. It is the innocence, affection, trust. A missionary who had tried to serve India but was aware of his failures and inadequacies told how one day when he was busy writing there darted past him a little seven-year-old Indian girl who had been playing with his own small daughter. As they came near, the Indian girl paused shyly, came up to him, passed her little brown hand across his cheek, and said, 'Your face is very dear to me.' He said afterwards that his heart was warm at that moment. He had given to India but in the giving he was receiving from the hand of a small child.

46

Just a look at a happy child is to receive a blessing ourselves.

As we grow older, even when we are urged to give and wish to do so, we are all the time receiving. It may be materially. It meant a great deal to me when I was going to college to train for the ministry (and probably thought of myself as a giver) but when I was also wondering how I would meet the expenses of the first few weeks in college, to be given £2 (a great sum then) by my minister. And in the early days of my ministry, with a six-month-old daughter and no cash to spare I received a five-pound note from 'Two Well-wishers'. All through life I have received not only that kind of gift but counsel, encouragement, the benefit of other people's skills and examples, and in the busiest days the gifts have been there, often unknown to me. I learned once that in what was probably the busiest year of my life one of my oldest friends had prayed for me daily.

The old have much to give even as they receive. This is not always easy and some of them feel they are too frail to give, while others may think of themselves as having all the wisdom the world needs. I have never forgotten how throughout my ministry I was supported and often guided by the experience and concern of older people, sometimes the 'shut-ins'. I enjoyed ministering to them; they gave so much to me.

Personal Giving

All this suggests that the highest giving and the greatest receiving are personal. It is ourselves we must give through counsel, skill or money. The apostle Paul was more pastor than theologian, and this was well put by him when he wrote to the Thessalonians:

> So, being affectionately desirous of you, we were ready to share with you not only the gospel of God, *but also our own selves*, because you had become very dear to us.[47]

This same stress on mutual giving and receiving at the personal level is found in his words to the Romans, 'I long to see you, that I may impart to you some spiritual gift to strengthen you, that is, that we may be mutually encouraged by each other's faith, both yours and mine.'[48] In the end it is people that we receive, and without this personal involvement all our giving is inadequate. The words of Bishop Azariah of India to the Edinburgh Conference of Churches in 1910 have often been quoted:

> Through all the ages to come the Indian Church will rise up in gratitude to attest the heroism and self-denying labours of the missionary body. You have given us your goods to feed the poor. You have given us your bodies to be burned. We also ask for *love*. Give us *friends*.

Seasons of giving and receiving are not only inextricably mixed. At the best we give and receive at the same time. We frequently hear those who have given prodigally and with distinction say that they have received more than they gave. It is the cry of the lover. Which of us has ever deserved the love we receive, even though we offer love? Without this sense of mutuality our giving becomes superior and we go on expecting to receive. One of the penalties of the Welfare State is that many come to take it for granted. State care was desperately needed, as those who lived through years of limited social security know, but the emphasis on what we should receive easily leads us to believe that the world owes us a living; we do not need to respond. Half a century ago I read a novel, the content of which I have entirely forgotten excepting for the vivid picture of a character I noted at the time:

> She did not receive life with open arms. . . . She held out her hands and received without the giving of thanks, and the good things of life came to her easily, without demand and seemingly without required payment. Life held no expectations but numberless gratifications. She had continually the air of one who might truly say, I brought everything into this world with me and I shall take everything out.[49]

The cure of this kind of selfishness is most of all to be found in the fact that God does far more for us than we can ever do for him. The amazing truth of the Christian faith is that we can never find God by our own efforts or know his power simply through our own searching.

I sought the Lord, and afterward I knew
    He moved my soul to seek him, seeking me;
It was not I that found, O Saviour true—
    No, I was found of thee.

Thou didst stretch forth thy hand and mine enfold;
    I walked and sank not on the storm-vexed sea.—
'Twas not so much that I on thee took hold,
    As thou, dear Lord, on me.

I find, I walk, I love, but O the whole
    Of love is but my answer, Lord, to thee;
For thou wert long beforehand with my soul,
    Alway thou lovest me.[50]

Breaking Down and Building Up

We praise and bless thee, gracious Lord,
  Our saviour kind and true,
For all the old things passed away,
  For all thou hast made new.

The old security is gone
  In which so long we lay;
The sleep of death thou hast dispelled,
  The darkness rolled away.

But yet how much must be destroyed,
  How much renewed must be,
Ere we can fully stand complete
  In likeness, Lord, to thee.

Karl Spitta, CP 404

And the Lord said: 'Because this people draw near with their
mouth and honour me with their lips while their hearts are far
from me, and their fear of me is a commandment of men learned
by rote; therefore, behold, I will again do marvellous things with
this people, wonderful and marvellous; and the wisdom of their
wise men shall perish, and the discernment of their discerning
men shall be hid. . . . And those who err in spirit will come to
understanding, and those who murmur will accept instruction.'

Isaiah 29:13, 14; 24

A boy was born mid little things,
  Between a little world and sky,
And dreamed not of the cosmic rings
  Round which the circling planets fly.
He lived in little works and thoughts,
  Where little ventures grow and plod,
And paced and ploughed his little plots
  And prayed unto his little God.
But as the mighty system grew
  His faith grew faint with many scars,
The cosmos widened in his view,
  But God was lost among the stars.

Another boy in lowly days,
  As he, to little things was born
But gathered lore in woodland ways
  And from the glory of the morn.
As wider skies broke on his view
  God greatened in his growing mind;
Each year he dreamed his God anew
  And left his older God behind.
He saw the boundless scheme dilate,
  In star and blossom, sky and clod,
And as the universe grew great,
  He dreamed for it a greater God.

SIX

Breaking Down and Building Up

It has been pointed out by commentators that three of the pairs in our passage from Ecclesiastes deal with the creative and the destructive elements of life.

A time to plant, and a time to pluck up what is planted;
A time to kill, and a time to heal;
A time to break down, and a time to build up.

I have already dealt with the commonly accepted meaning of the first of these, the giving in planting and the receiving in harvest. Uprooting or Harvest is also used figuratively of destroying a nation. If these passages are used metaphorically then 'kill' also may be taken as referring to destruction. Healing also is not only to be thought of medically.

> The widespread figurative uses of these verbs strongly suggest they were chosen here to express not only specific activities but all the manifold pursuits of men, creative and destructive, good and evil, benevolent and malevolent.[51]

I see these passages therefore as a reminder that there are seasons of breaking down and seasons of building up.

I have said a good deal about maturity and a part of our life must always be a seeking to build and to achieve that maturity. But this is not simply a matter of adding something to the past building. Sometimes it means the destruction of the old so that better things may come.

This has been seen in the changes of cities and towns, as old slum properties have made way for new, sometimes high-rise, buildings. It has not always been for the better and often the new quickly becomes as bad as or worse than the old but destruction inevitably precedes new building and often when the old has gone we are glad. What replaces it is so much better. I have seen a wilderness destroyed and new, well-built houses replace it. Whether this is for good or ill depends upon the values and skills of the planners, the architects, the builders, and also upon the aims of society.

You may see the twofold action also in the development of our physical bodies. I do not know if it is still claimed that the constituents of our bodies change completely every seven years, but we cannot become fully grown without the destruction of at least some of the earlier make-up. The milk teeth of the small child will go and will be replaced by the more varied and stronger teeth of the older child and adult, better able to fulfil the joys and duties of eating!

We see this also in the development of our knowledge. Much that we first learn is simple, direct, uncomplicated and though it is sufficient at the time, we need a greater knowledge later. Often we seem to build on what we already know but there come times when we must question and replace what we once held as true. I am quite sure that the physics and chemistry I learned at school would not enable me to share in the scientific scene today. Some of the assumptions we then had have gone, to be replaced by a new understanding. This is true of many branches of knowledge. The study of a living language of the past is often influenced by the discovery of old documents which show that some words were used in a different way from what was generally accepted, or further study reveals that references which were interpreted in one way must be seen as meaning something different. This has been a great factor in the study of the New Testament. The study of the ideas and philosophies of the day, as undertaken for example by Dr C. H. Dodd, have assisted the understanding of the background of Christ's day and Paul's world, and the discovery of papyri in the sands of Egypt brought home to scholars new meanings for words used in the Greek of the New Testament. These discoveries have supported the view that the language of the New Testament was the common speech of the time and not a special language. Some interesting illustrations are given in

E. C. Hoskyns and N. Davey's *The Riddle of the New Testament*:[52]

> The Prodigal Son did not vaguely 'gather together' all his share of his father's substance; he 'realised' it, converted it into ready money. St Paul had not heard that some of the Thessalonians were 'walking disorderly' but they were 'playing truant', not going to work, in expectation of the imminent end of the world. Judas carried the 'money-box', not the bag.

Such discoveries have sometimes seemed like a destruction of the old and a rebuilding that is new.

This spreads to the Christian faith in a personal sense. Much that we learned as children about the faith will remain with us all our lives, and for this we can be grateful. But we also learn wrong ideas and as we grow older they cannot carry us through. All too often we are afraid of questioning, let alone discarding our earlier convictions, and for some the destroying of the old and the creating of the new brings deep anguish. An example is seen in Edmund Gosse's *Father and Son*, first published in 1907. Gosse's parents were Plymouth Brethren with very rigid views about religion and behaviour. Edmund Gosse describes how there was between him and his father 'a struggle between two temperaments, two consciences and almost two epochs. It ended, as was inevitable, in disruption. Of the two human beings here described, one was born to fly backward, the other could not help being carried forward.'[53] He called his book the 'diagnosis of a dying Puritanism' relating how in his life he had to destroy the rigidities his father had tried to instil in him, that he might build a new independence in faith. It was an extremely painful experience. The fact is, however, that it has often been through this journey of destruction that some have come to a more mature faith. The skill of some preachers and teachers is that they can destroy the non-essential and build the essential.

No one who has served the Emmanuel Church in Cambridge during the past half century can be unaware of the tremendous influence of Henry Carter, minister there for thirty-five years. I once asked a friend who had worshipped in the church as a student what was the secret of Mr Carter's power. He mentioned several aspects of his ministry and then went on to describe his preaching. He said it was as though he gently and deliberately knocked away all the props and false ideas you had and then helped to rebuild a new and larger faith. In a day when so many find it easy to destroy faith I long for more of that kind of teaching and preaching. The destruction must often have been painful and some may never have recovered from it but how wonderful could be the rebuilt and richer house of faith.

This theme of seasons of breaking down and building up may be followed in various ways in the life of the Church. Churches have often become more and more wedded to their buildings and many of their problems are related to these same premises. Often they must go. Even if we had the money we could not repair and restore them so they have to be destroyed. Rebuilding enables the local congregation to have a home suited to its mission, possibly to have a suite of buildings which includes houses or rooms of service to the community, sometimes also giving an income which helps meet the cost of the new sanctuary and rooms for the work of the church. In some cases the church will never be rebuilt on the same site. It may close as people move elsewhere, or it may unite with another congregation of the same or of a different denomination. The story can be traced in what has happened with particular denominations in London. Many inner-city churches closed and were never rebuilt but were replaced by churches in the suburbs, gradually going further out. There was loss as well as gain and today we rightly insist that there should be a policy which includes rebuilding in the inner cities. Nevertheless the old buildings have often had to be destroyed. We are still seeking to find the right replacements. The change has not been without pain and disagreement.

We see these seasons also in the witness and missionary task of the Church. At home many of those outside the Church have false ideas about what the

Church believes concerning faith and practice and before we can hope to convince them of the truth of the Gospel we may have to help them destroy their false beliefs. They will quote to us from the Old Testament the ideas of God and man they have discovered there without seeming to realise that God has made himself more fully known in Jesus Christ. The God who commanded Saul to destroy the Amalekites[54] cannot speak to us as can the One who sent his Son to save the world. Jesus made quite clear that he had come to destroy much, that he might build anew. 'You have heard that it was said, "You shall love your neighbour and hate your enemy." But I say to you, Love your enemies and pray for those who persecute you, so that you may be sons of your Father who is in heaven.' Indeed the whole of Matthew chapter 5 speaks of what must be destroyed[55] so that a great faith may arise. That does not mean that we contrast the whole of the Old Testament with the whole of the New, for in the Old there are, eg in Moses and the prophets, signs of a richer understanding. To move to the present time, many (sometimes within as well as outside the Church) will believe that the purpose of life is to achieve one's own prosperity and to find happiness in self-satisfaction, with no control or discipline. To correct false impressions, to share the faith and to build is a part of our missionary task today, and it is a costly task as it covers breaking and building.

The Life of the Church

The two seasons are further discovered in the development of the life of the Church. Many say that the Church is such a conservative body that it never changes. We know the truth of the accusation and that often we give the impression that we stay just as we were but the claim is only partly true. Look back at the story of the Church and you will see how greatly it has changed through the centuries, from the house churches of the New Testament to the great cathedrals and preaching centres; and for us as Nonconformists from the buildings tucked away in corners so that they could not be seen by those who would harm them, to the huge Victorian structures, and now to the more simple, limited and dual-purpose buildings frequently the home of several denominations, and in some cases a return to the house churches. Always the building of the one follows the destruction of the former buildings.

We may also see it in the worship and in the pattern of our services. In the United Reformed Church we do not have the argument about the Alternative Service Book replacing the Cranmer Prayer Book but we have our changes. It has come in the language we use. God is now probably more frequently addressed as 'You' than as 'Thou'. Sermons are considerably shorter than they were fifty years ago. Where evening services were once the better attended now it is the morning service which brings the larger congregation. All this may seem insignificant and often is a reaction to changed social conditions, but a more searching examination of the life of the churches will show that much has been destroyed in the pattern of the Church's activities. We may see this particularly in the work among children. For the greater part of the story of the Church there was little special provision since children shared in worship with their parents. In the eighteenth century there came in this country the founding of Sunday Schools. Readers of Trollope's Barchester novels will know how bitterly this was opposed by some. A great change came at the beginning of the present century with the Graded Sunday Schools, and in the past fifty years there has been the Family Church emphasis in varying forms, seeking to promote once more the unity in worship and in teaching. In each change there has been destruction and creation. Now we seem to be drifting. Is there something that has yet to be destroyed that there may be a better form of caring for the children and young people? Sometimes I sigh for the creative imagination of a Robert Raikes (who founded Sunday Schools), a Hamilton Archibald (who did so much for the grading of schools and the training of workers among the young), of a Herbert Hamilton (who introduced into Congregationalism the ideas of Family

Church). Anyone who shared in their visions would probably destroy much that we now have and build a better Church, different in form but one in essential purpose.

Here is a theme to explore further but all talk of destruction and rebuilding has its dangers. Destruction can be careless, destroying the good with the bad, brutal and badly carried out. It needs skill and care if it is to be replaced by something better. I have been watching the clearing of a site for a local development. At first the clearing seemed almost indiscriminate, but in fact it was well planned and carried through with wisdom, for the breaking down and the building must at best be seen not as two seasons but as one. So it is with the challenge and the renewing of faith. Henry Carter of Cambridge did not simply challenge false ideas. Some of his hearers may have missed the next sermon on rebuilding, if the first had only destroyed. He would have seen the two movements as one. As the destruction calls for planning and efficiency so does the rebuilding. We need to know our goal, lest to us there be applied the damning word, 'This man began to build, and was not able to finish.'[56]

There remains much to be broken down in the world—false gods, false values, malice, and so many unlovely things.

> But yet how much must be destroyed,
>   How much renewed must be,
> Ere we can fully stand complete
>   In likeness, Lord, to thee.

We were taught to see the kingdom of God as a gift; we cannot build it; yet there is a sense in which we are called to be workers within the kingdom, seeing the old order changing and God fulfilling himself in many ways.

War and Peace

We the Peoples of the United Nations, determined to save succeeding generations from the scourge of war, which twice in our lifetime has brought untold sorrow to mankind, and to reaffirm faith in fundamental human rights, in the dignity and worth of the human person, in the equal rights of men and women and of nations large and small, and to establish conditions under which justice and respect for the obligations arising from treaties and other sources of international law can be maintained, and to promote social progress and better standards of life in larger freedom, and for these ends, to practise tolerance and live together in peace with one another as good neighbours, and to unite our strength to maintain international peace and security, and to ensure by the acceptance of principles and the institution of methods, that armed force shall not be used, save in the common interest, and to employ international machinery for the promotion of the economic and social advancement of all peoples, have resolved to combine our efforts to accomplish these aims. . . .

Preamble to the United Nations Charter, 1945.

It is far easier to make war than to make peace.

Georges Clemenceau, 1919.

Lead me from death to life, from falsehood to truth
Lead me from despair to hope, from fear to trust
Lead me from hate to love, from war to peace
Let peace fill our heart, our world, our universe . . .
Peace — Peace — Peace.

Prayer for Peace, June 1982.

It shall come to pass in the latter days that the mountain of the house of the Lord shall be established as the highest of the mountains, and shall be raised up above the hills; and peoples shall flow to it, and many nations shall come and say: 'Come, let us go up to the mountain of the Lord, to the house of the God of Jacob; that he may teach us his ways and we may walk in his paths.' For out of Zion shall go forth the law, and the word of the Lord from Jerusalem. He shall judge between many peoples, and shall decide for strong nations afar off; and they shall beat their swords into ploughshares, and their spears into pruning hooks; nation shall not lift up sword against nation, neither shall they learn war any more.

Micah 4:1-3.

SEVEN

War and Peace

I find myself recoiling from the last of the dual seasons of Ecclesiastes, 'a time for war, and a time for peace'. Can there ever be a time when there must be war, and dare we speak as though war and peace were of equal importance? These queries would not have been thought of by the writer. He looked at the world and saw that there were times when the nations went to war and days when they had peace, and probably to him, in this passage, peace was simply the absence of war. So it had been long before his day. So it is in the main in the Old Testament. Indeed, in the second book of Samuel we read, 'In the spring of the year, the time when kings go forth to battle, David sent Joab, and his servants with him, and all Israel; and they ravaged the Ammonites, and besieged Rabbah.'[57] It is described as though it were a kind of harvest, and the troops were sent out to work in the fields. Presumably the winter was not a time for war; fighting would be even more uncomfortable then. War was thought of as essential by patriarch and king, psalmist and prophet. It was often waged at what was seen as God's command in order to fulfil his purpose. There were a few who looked further, to the time when war would be no more, such as Isaiah and Micah,[58] but that was a distant dream, soon obscured by other battles and by wars between nations and the struggle within the nation itself.

Peace also mattered a great deal, and there are few lovelier words than the Hebrew 'Shalom'. It meant the absence of war when they could settle down and rebuild and their children could grow up without fear; but it meant more than that. The word includes all that we mean by welfare and it also refers to the victory of God's purposes. It speaks to the whole of life, indeed the very word 'Shalom' refers to wholeness. The prophets looked to the time when peace would overwhelm war.

In the New Testament war is still seen as a fact in life. Jesus himself used illustrations from war. This does not mean that he approved of war. In Luke he is speaking of his need to assess the consequences of the spiritual battle he was waging. 'What king, going to encounter another king in war, will not sit down first and take counsel whether he is able with ten thousand to meet him who comes against him with twenty thousand?'[59] The real battle was in the heart, and Jesus is pointing to the costly victory to be won within. 'So therefore, whoever of you does not renounce all that he has cannot be my disciple.' Jesus develops what had begun in the Old Testament; he shifts the emphasis from the battle without to the war within. Wars come from the human heart. What comes out of a man defiles him. James in his letter took up the theme: 'What causes wars, and what causes fightings among you? Is it not your passions that are at war in your members?'[60] So there is in the New Testament a greater stress on peace, a season that must never end. To Jesus and his followers, peace is a relationship with God and with each other. It is given by God through Christ. 'Peace I leave with you; my peace I give to you.'[61] Peace was therefore a personal relationship with Christ. As it was to be expressed in the letter to the Ephesians, 'For (Christ) is our peace, who has made us both one, and has broken down the dividing wall of hostility.'[62] When we share the peace at a communion service or the word is used in blessing at the end of worship, we know that the season of peace is greater than that of war.

Yet the seasons remain and the language is used. In the last book of the Bible there are several references to war, the best known being the war that arose in heaven.[63] The greatest battle for the Christian is often seen in the human heart. In that area God himself wages war.

> Then, God of truth, for whom we long,
>   Thou who wilt hear our prayer,
> Do thine own battle in our hearts,
>   And slay the falsehood there.[64]

We are aware of that continually waged battle. If we

would destroy war and all its attendant evils we must become men and women of peace. However strongly we oppose modern warfare, our opposition will mean little if hatred and war are in our own hearts.

Anger

This raises the question whether it is ever right for us to be angry with others when we realise that anger can cause untold harm. Anger, however, has a place in every life. It has been said that 'anger is one of the sinews of the soul; he who lacks it hath a maimed mind'. The Bible often speaks of anger with approval. Jesus himself was angry, not because of the ill-treatment he suffered but because of the harm he saw being done to others, frequently in the name of religion. In the synagogue he was angry when the Pharisees would have allowed a man to continue to suffer rather than be healed on the Sabbath. 'He looked around at them with anger, grieved at their hardness of heart.'[65] There is a splendid chapter in H. E. Fosdick's *The Manhood of the Master* on 'The Master's Indignation'. Powerfully he writes:

Let it be said with distinctness that love like that of the Master is terrible. It looks on Lazarus—*and then it looks on Dives!* It looks on the little children in the factory—and then on the men who profit by their labour and on the society that allows the outrage. . . . A feeble and negative benignity can observe these wrongs to men and be unstirred, but a positive love, like the Master's, is roused from its depths with indignation. His words flame up with that scathing power which profound passion alone can give.[66]

There are seasons when our souls must be completely free from anger but there are also seasons when anger is a right response to the evils of the world. The great difficulty is to discover the right season. Said George Matheson, the hymn writer, 'There are times when I do well to be angry, but I have mistaken the times.' We have to take to ourselves the question put to Jonah, 'Do you do well to be angry?'[67]

61

Anger and War

Anger may be a Christian virtue at times but how do we express it? What are we to do about a strong nation that oppresses a weaker people? Here is one of the perpetual struggles for men and women of peace, and particularly for the Christian. We ask again and again if it can ever be right to prepare for war or to try to settle disputes by war. When we look back it seems that there have indeed been times for war and times for peace, of which we must all take note. It is often pointed out that in the first part of this century war and peace on a large scale succeeded each other and we are reminded that as far as Great Britain goes we have now had more than forty years without a major war, though there have been battles elsewhere, war in the Falklands, internal strife and terrorism in Ireland, the Middle East and India and Africa. If these be not war as some would define it, they are hardly seasons of peace. Through all these years mounting sums of money have been spent on preparing for war, when it is so desperately needed to help feed, house and educate millions. We can never be content with the thought of seasons of war as well as peace.

There may still be a few who believe that war is a means of keeping the population in check, and there are others who point out with truth the virtues that have been developed in war—courage, intelligence, concern for others—they have all gone along with warfare. Ernest Renan, a French scholar and historian, wrote in 1871, 'War is, in a sense, one condition of progress, the whip cut preventing a country from going to sleep and forcing satisfied mediocrity to shake off its apathy.'[68] It is often suggested also that a spell in the forces and experience of warfare would help cure hooliganism experienced at football matches and in the inner cities. I find that difficult to believe. It may well be, however, that dependence upon war and the increasing violence of the day are connected.

The End of War

We cannot lightly accept the division into seasons of

war and peace. The true battle is a spiritual one and war is one of the greatest enemies. We aim at a lasting peace which is also wholeness of life and includes all that we understand by welfare together with inner serenity. But how may we hope to achieve that peace? One obvious and clearly expressed view is that we can do away with war only by being strong, stronger than others. Potential enemies must know that our nation could do great damage if threatened or attacked. The opposite view is that war can never outlaw war and that it is in itself wrong. The pacifist has so declared for a long time. Today the emphasis in opposition to war is more on outlawing its worst forms. Ban the bomb. Seek nuclear disarmament or at least a nuclear freeze. Whether this is sufficiently radical I would doubt but we need to encourage all we can the attempts to limit, and ultimately to do away with, the preparations for war.

This is no easy decision to make. In the end it has to include individual decisions. In the years leading up to the second world war I saw many struggling with this question as I had to myself. When war came some who had been pacifist felt compelled to change their position in the face of Nazi oppression. They did not do so easily. There were others who felt they had to say 'no'. They often suffered greatly, not only from the scorn of those who supported the war but because they found themselves separated from friends with whom they wished to be united. It is true that provision was made for conscientious objectors but the pain was still there. So there was anguish on both sides. Today, when the situation has changed and war, if it comes, will be much more mechanical and less personal, we see the battle in many hearts. The struggle and the pain must continue. There can be no lasting season that is right for war but there may still in fact be war. All the time we know that war must be outlawed in our own hearts and we look for a season when:

> No longer hosts encountering hosts
> Their millions slain deplore;

> They hang the trumpet in the hall,
> And study war no more.[69]

Disobedience and Violence

Seasons of war and peace may also be seen inside a nation and a more pressing problem for some is the extent to which civil disobedience, even violence, is justified. While most of us are law-abiding we who are within the Nonconformist tradition know that freedom of worship was purchased through disobedience and at one time our forefathers promoted civil war. We look at the world now and find, for example, that in South Africa there is civil disobedience encouraged by the churches whom many of us would support since we believe apartheid to be utterly unchristian. There are similar situations in other countries. There are many who feel that passive opposition is not enough and they turn to violence. I cannot so interpret the Christian faith. Behind these struggles is also the question of law and order. Writing to the Romans when Christians were already meeting persecution, the apostle Paul said:

> Let every person be subject to the governing authorities. For there is no authority except from God. Therefore he who resists the authorities resists what God has appointed, and those who resist will incur judgment. For rulers are not a terror to good conduct, but to bad. . . . If you do wrong, be afraid, for he does not bear the sword in vain.[70]

The whole chapter where this is found needs further study. I wonder how these words would be taken by those who today live under an oppressive regime. The first Christians themselves had to suffer persecution and knew that they could not always obey the demands of the state. Paul was to die as a martyr because to him Christ was above all earthly rulers. I take this passage from Romans as asserting that government is essential. Anarchy can never be Christian. Yet rulers themselves are subject to God. For ourselves we need to have very strong reasons for disobeying the law. In the past it has proved to be right but as I look back it seems to me that it was not so much the violence of the Civil War in the seventeenth century that gave us freedom of worship as the witness of those who refused to accept the laws that governed their way of worship in the years before and after that war. Today as then there are matters in all countries of conscience and of disturbance of spirit. We have no right lightly to judge one another.

What can we learn through the seasons of war and peace, especially that of war? There are those who look back with nostalgia at their days in the forces in wartime. Some good things came to them yet the sadness and the evil predominate, and the aftermath of any war is likely to be dangerous. Nevertheless Ecclesiastes was talking of seasons that actually happened and war has been a fact we cannot ignore. Indeed great discoveries, psychological as well as scientific in a more general sense, have been made when nations were at war. In the second world war I recall how wonderfully people of different views learned to work together. A Penguin paperback special, *Is Christ Divided?*, showed how pacifist and non-pacifist could do so, and how the churches were being brought together across denominational and national boundaries. At a different level I found that in such a time of tragedy and searching the faith of men and women was deepened even as in some cases it was threatened. Dr R. F. Horton's words about the gains in his ministry at Hampstead during the first world war expressed for me how I felt in a season of war which in itself was so harmful.

If I am permitted to live through the war and to look back upon it as an event in the past, I believe I shall regard it as the most fruitful period of my ministry. When the Church seemed to melt away . . . when people were so overstrained that they could not listen to sermons, and grumbled, in the same breath, that they would not go to church because they got no teaching, and because they could not listen to the teaching they got; when everything had become unnatural, feverish, aguish, through the anxieties which pressed upon the public mind; and when even the kindest friends and loyalest members of the Church were always complaining that the Church had missed her opportunity; ... in that time of almost unimaginable difficulty, it was an unspeakable mercy to be allowed to go on week by week, whether people would listen or not, whether they criticised or were indifferent, declaring that God was over all, and that the issue would be right ... and that through all our blindness and blundering, our suffering and sin, there was the everlasting Gospel of Jesus and his love.[71]

In some respects times have not changed.

Sombre Seasons

He will destroy on this mountain the covering that is cast over all peoples, the veil that is spread over all nations. He will swallow up death for ever, and *The Lord God will wipe away tears from all faces*, and the reproach of his people he will take away from all the earth; for the Lord has spoken.

Isaiah 25:7, 8

From all faces, from your face and my face,
From white, pink, red, black, brown and yellow faces.
From young faces, old faces, soft, hard and tender faces,
He will wipe away tears.
He will wipe away tears. Tears will come and he will wipe
    them away.
Tears that have come, tears that hurt, tears that cleanse,
    tears that renew,
Tears that cut into life as a stream into a hillside,
Tears that must come down,
and the Lord will wipe them away.

From *Council for World Mission Handbook,* 1980

It has often seemed to me that, if we do not know at first hand the meaning of real suffering, we are missing something of the essential human experience. Somewhere in a novel—I can't remember where it is—there is a passage in which a mother tells her daughter how she has always tried to shield her from suffering. She expects gratitude, but is aghast at the girl's stricken cry, 'But I claim the *right* to suffer!'

Leslie J. Tizard, *Facing Life and Death*

If he could speak, that victim torn and bleeding,
    Caught in his pain and nailed upon the cross,
Has he to give the comfort souls are needing?
    Could he destroy the bitterness of loss?

Peace does not mean the end of all our striving,
    Joy does not mean the drying of our tears;
Peace is the power that comes to souls arriving
    Up to the light where God himself appears.

Give me, for light, the sunshine of thy sorrow,
    Give me, for shelter, shadow of thy cross;
Give me to share the glory of thy morrow,
    Gone from my heart the bitterness of loss.

Studdart Kennedy, *The Suffering God*

EIGHT

Sombre Seasons

I have indicated that not all the seasons of Ecclesiastes are imediately attractive. The mixture of the happy and the sad is seen when he speaks of 'a time to weep, and a time to laugh'. In this chapter I write specially about weeping, but I would never lose sight of the seasons of laughter. It is a poor life if we have no time to laugh. Few judgments on the life of Jesus are so wildly wrong as that of Swinburne, 'Thou hast conquered, O pale Galilean; the world has grown grey with thy breath.'[72] In his own day Jesus was not always thought of as the man of sorrows. He was accused of being a glutton and a drunkard, because of the company he kept and the joy that was in his life. He contrasted his own way of life with the more dour picture of John the Baptist,[73] and he spoke of the joy he knew, a joy he passed on to others. 'These things I have spoken to you, that my joy may be in you, and that your joy may be full.'[74] Compassionate and thoughtful people often become so obsessed with the problems and burdens of the world that they cannot see the good and the joyful. Geoffrey Ainger, in his book *Jesus our Contemporary*, written from the heart of Notting Hill, inner London, saw Jesus as 'The Justified Celebrant', the man who was happy, and he tells a story of Karl Barth who had tried to work out a positive theology through two wars, and who now lectured to students in the university of Bonn at seven o'clock in the morning, 'always after we had sung a hymn to cheer ourselves up'. Then he spoke to students 'with their grave faces, which had still to learn to smile again'. This over-emphasis on the sadness of the world easily leads to helplessness and to cynicism. Sometimes when I meet married couples solemnly examining every aspect of their behaviour towards each other I want to say, 'Laugh, perhaps *at* each other, certainly *with* each other.'

A Sad World

I would not wish for a moment to minimise the sorrows of life. These seasons are so varied. They were well expressed by Leslie Tizard in an address from the chair of the Congregational Union:

How many people there are stumbling under a burden of guilt—often a morbid, exaggerated sense of guilt fastened upon them in early childhood when, in truth, they were innocent enough! How many are tortured by vague, nameless anxieties! ... Who can compute the depression and irritability, the sense of failure, the crippling feeling of inferiority which makes life a misery for many?[75]

That was said over thirty years ago but it is still true, even though we often try to hide it. He was speaking of the work of the pastor and in one sense the range of his concern was limited. We need to go much further into life's pain. The sorrows of the world, the years of defeat, the pangs of hunger, the horror of loneliness and homelessness may make us feel that the times of weeping are more than the seasons of laughter. Fortunately not all feel that way. Cheerfulness is for ever breaking through.

Jesus Wept

We look more closely into the seasons of weeping. Jesus knew them. Twice he is recorded as weeping, though not for himself. He wept for a friend, Lazarus, who had died; and he wept for his own people. Among the most memorable moments for me in two visits to the Holy Land were opportunities to stand in the chapel Dominus Flevit (Jesus wept) and look over Jerusalem. The spot where Jesus stood as he had come round a bend from Bethany must have been just here. 'And when he drew near and saw the city he wept over it, saying, Would that even today you knew the things that make for peace! But now they are hid from your eyes.'[76] His heart was near to breaking and at that moment we see in him a concentration of sorrow leading to the cross. Something of that overwhelming compassion is found in many others and we all need it, to be able to weep with them that weep. That kind of weeping may well lead us on to care for others.

As Jesus looked at Jerusalem and recalled the repeated disobedience of the Jewish people he must have been feeling how many were the opportunities they had wasted. H. H. Farmer wrote in *Towards Belief in God:*

> There is . . . no situation in life in which the question of waste, the question, what is it all for? is not, if we may so put it, just round the corner. Even in the most zestful activities, those whose intrinsic excitement and interest seem to be their own sufficient justification, this is so. Particularly as we get older the question has a way of suddenly poking out its head and peering round the corner at us, of coming out of the wings and mingling in the business of the stage or, at any rate, of making disconcerting 'noises off', of blowing a gust of cold air across even the pleasantest picnic.[77]

We might go much further in tracing waste in the world and in our own lives and while apportioning blame, probably mainly to other people, we could also have the feeling that this is a part of life over which we have no control. And indeed there is bound to be some waste in life and this could partly have been in the mind of Ecclesiastes when he wrote of 'a time to cast away stones, and a time to gather stones together'.

Our Own Fault?

While there is weeping for the sorrows of the world and the waste and suffering in our own lives as well, with an awareness of our personal weaknesses, there is also a weeping for our own failure and self-made anguish. So we sense the deep misery in Peter when 'he went out and wept bitterly' after denying that he knew Jesus.[78] Were there not also tears in the eyes and weeping in the heart of Judas when he realised how he had betrayed his Master even to death?[79] The knowledge of our past sins haunts us and brings painful regret. Perhaps even worse is when we do not admit our share in the evils of life, the ways in which we deny our Lord.

71

> I have denied thee, Master, not in fright
> And weakness bred of sudden dread;
> I have denied thee when my heart was light.
>
> I have denied thee, and my sin was deep;
> Not in my creeds, but in my deeds
> I have denied thee—and I did not weep.[80]

Inevitably this concern with waste and with our own failures leads us to ask what are the causes of grief. In the sombre seasons there is much that we can do, and we could in ourselves remove a large part of the accumulated sorrow, as is being done by those rushing at the present time to relieve the starving and homeless people of Ethiopia. We can also tackle our own sorrows more courageously than we sometimes do. There is a tendency among some of us as Christians to make a burden of things which non-Christians pass over lightly. We may feel deeply, but we can also cherish self-pity. Obviously, however, the evils that happen to us and those in the world around are not always our fault, and it is equally foolish for us to blame ourselves. How many parents lose their joy and think they are to blame when their children seem to them to take wrong roads? Even those who have surrounded their young with discriminating love and care are often disappointed. A certain realism is needed in these seasons if we are not to become quite useless. Nevertheless sorrows will remain.

Depression

Depression has been in the news in recent years, and needs to be spoken of with care. What we might describe as normal depression has been a fact throughout history. You will find it again and again in the psalms and in the prophets. Jeremiah deeply felt the way in which he was treated and the sense he had that even God had deserted him.[81] King Hezekiah, facing imminent death, cries, 'O Lord, I am oppressed; be thou my security!'[82] In Psalms 42 and 43 the feelings of anguish, of being deserted by God and man, are vividly expressed:

My tears have been my food day and night . . .
All thy waves and thy billows have gone over me . . .
Why are you cast down, O my soul,
and why are you disquieted within me?

Yet that is never the end. Read on, and in each case the depression passes. 'Hope in God: for I shall again praise him, my help and my God.' So it is with the depressed feelings of most of us. The nameless anxieties, the fears in the night, that sinking feeling which a particular night-time drink was once supposed to prevent, will in most cases disappear. Often the reason for the depression is some simple physical cause and a visit to the doctor may help, or a good friend may tease us out of our moaning or rebuke us for hanging on to sorrow and self-pity. Unfortunately that is not all. It is true that for many depression in the medical sense as it is now used is unknown. They believe that if they are depressed or fed-up they will come through, and it is sometimes hard for them to sympathise with people who have a depressive sickness. The onlooker finds it so much easier to say to the victim, 'Pull yourself together.' Yet this depression is not new. Long before the present technical descriptions of depression, deep-seated and peristent melancholy was known. One man who could be called a depressive was William Cowper. All through his life he had bouts of depression. Some were passing; others lasted a long time; and finally there was a collapse into 'unutterable despair'.[83] The story has been sympathetically told in *The Stricken Deer* by Lord David Cecil. The man who could write poems of gentle beauty and hymns which still speak to the spiritual experience of Christians could also be compelled to write to a friend, the Rev William Bull:

> Both your advice and your manner of giving it are gentle and friendly, and like yourself. I thank you for them, and do not refuse your counsel because it is not good, but because it is not for me; there is not a man upon earth that might not be the better for it, myself only excepted.[84]

He went on to say that there was no encouragement in

73

the scripture so comprehensive as to include his case. He could not rise from his deep sense of being lost.

Doubtless something more could be done for him today, as it is for many victims of depression. Skilled help is needed. It will include that of the psychiatrist or psychologist but it also includes the experienced and careful understanding of those who are able to offer care and cure in sorrow. The pastor, the wife or husband, the true friend—all may help. The sympathetic surrounding by the fellowship of a church has also done wonderful things. Those who watch often with deepening sorrow themselves can at least never give in, and we know that wonderful cures are taking place.

Persistent Pain

There are other sombre seasons which many share but which do not overwhelm so completely, though they may last for years, sometimes until death. Physical pain, changes in personal fortune, problems with other people, unemployment with no hope of a job, the ironies of life, all add to the feeling of loss and melancholy. Once more, friendship and the fellowship of a caring church will help.

Joy and Woe

Something more must be said, for you cannot separate completely the times to weep and the times to laugh. In the wholeness of the seasons there is winter as well as summer, and there would be no harvest without both. For most people, to achieve fullness of living there will be sorrow as well as joy; indeed they will have a false view of life if they try to shut out suffering. William Blake expressed it well:

> Man was made for joy and woe;
> And when this we rightly know
> Thro' the world we safely go.
> Joy and woe are woven fine,
> A clothing for the soul divine;
> Under every grief and pine
> Runs a joy with silken twine.[85]

It could be added that the help that some are able to give to others who live in the sombre seasons comes from their own grappling with sorrow, for they have discovered with the writer of Psalm 30 that 'weeping may tarry for the night, but joy comes with the morning'.

In the end, it is our attitude to life and our personal faith that will take us through the shadowed seasons. When C. S. Lewis wrote *The Problem of Pain* in 1940, he said in the Preface:

> The only purpose of the book is to solve the intellectual problem raised by suffering; for the far higher task of teaching fortitude and patience I was never fool enough to suppose myself qualified, nor have I anything to offer my readers except my conviction that when pain is to be borne, a little courage helps more than much knowledge, a little human sympathy more than much courage, and the least tincture of the love of God more than all.[86]

That takes us part of the way but a greater faith is available as Lewis discovered himself. Many have found that as they turn repeatedly towards Jesus, in his sufferings he is sharing theirs, and they are given strength. I have known those who have risen above their physical and mental pain, and their grief for others, and have shown that the sombre seasons are not destructive.

> Who is the angel that cometh?
>   Pain!
> Let us arise and go forth to greet him,
>   Not in vain
> Is the summons come for us to meet him;
> He will stay and darken our sun.
>   He will stay
>   A desolate night, a weary day.
> Since in his shadow our work is done,
> And in that shadow our crowns are won,
> Let us say still, while his bitter chalice
> Slowly into our hearts is poured,
>   'Blessed is he that cometh
>   In the name of the Lord.'[87]

A Time to Die

Then I saw a new heaven and a new earth; for the first heaven and the first earth had passed away, and the sea was no more. And I saw the holy city, new Jerusalem, coming down out of heaven from God, prepared as a bride adorned for her husband; and I heard a great voice from the throne saying, 'Behold, the dwelling of God is with men. He will dwell with them, and they shall be his people, and God himself will be with them; he will wipe away every tear from their eyes, and death shall be no more, neither shall there be mourning nor crying nor pain any more, for the former things have passed away.'

And he who sat upon the throne said, 'Behold, I make all things new.' . . .

And I saw no temple in the city, for its temple is the Lord God the Almighty and the Lamb. And the city has no need of sun or moon to shine upon it, for the glory of God is its light, and its lamp is the Lamb.

Revelation 21:1-5; 22, 23

> If I should go before the rest of you
> Break not a flower nor inscribe a stone,
> Nor when I'm gone speak in a Sunday voice
> But be the usual selves that I have known.
>> Weep if you must,
>> Parting is hell,
>> But life goes on,
>> So sing as well.

Joyce Grenfell, quoted in *Joyce*

It is so delicious to be *done* with things, and to feel no need any longer to concern myself much about earthly affairs. I seem on the verge of a most delightful journey to a place of unknown joys and pleasures, and things here seem of so little importance compared to things there, that they have lost most of their interest for me.

I cannot describe the sort of done-with-the-world feeling I have. It is not that I feel as if I was going to die at all, but simply that the world seems to me nothing but a passage way to the real life beyond; and passage ways are very unimportant places. . . .

My wants seem to be gradually narrowing down, my *personal* wants, I mean. . . . I do not know whether this is piety or old age, or a little of each mixed together, but honestly the world and our life in it does seem of too little account to be worth making the least fuss over, when one has such a magnificent prospect ahead of one; and I am tremendously content to let one activity after another go, and to await quietly and happily the opening of the door at the end of the passage way, that will let me in to my real abiding place.

A letter from Mrs Pearsall Smith, *A Religious Rebel*

NINE

A Time to Die

I have been writing of the clarity of the seasons, the definite demarcation between day and night, between Advent and Lent. I have also indicated that sometimes the seasons seem to get confused. A bright morning is followed by a dull afternoon, when the light vanishes. The seasons get muddled in our minds, and distinctions disappear. This may be because of some new inner experience. 'It's June in January, all because I'm in love!' The rhythm one regarded as permanently established may be broken in other ways. Travel makes it possible to have a summer in winter-time. Refrigeration gives to us food 'out of season'. Unemployment may make a regular rhythm impossible. Marriage and the birth of children notoriously alter established habits. Conversion either to a new faith or within an old faith may change the pattern of days and weeks.

Nevertheless the basic need for rhythm remains. Sometimes the rhythm of the past will be recovered after long absence. New patterns of life will be created in the use of each day but it will be a new 'rhythm'. When changes take place it is probably good to remind people that there is always the danger of becoming set in one's ways, so that the new rhythm becomes a prison as much as the earlier way of life. In all the talk of seasons, allow for the new surprises which each day may bring.

There will inevitably come a time when the seasons we know vanish. There will be no spring and summer, no day and night, no weekday or Sunday. The whole round of life will have been completed as far as we know it. This Ecclesiastes had in mind when he wrote of 'a time to be born, and a time to die'. All his book is concerned with the facts of life. Death was the end. Read the pages of near despair and the conclusion that we must make the best of the season in which we live: 'Whatever your hand finds to do, do it with your might; for there is no work or thought or knowledge or wisdom in Sheol (the grave) to which you are going.'[88]

But what shall we say of death? It has been said that the great unmentionable in the Victorian times was sex, and that in this century it is death. I do not believe that is quite so true today as it was earlier in the century. The magnificent work of hostels for the dying reveals a readiness to accept that death must come. There is however still a reluctance to go and see a doctor when terminal illness is feared, and the refusal or the delay of many in making a will is there because they will not face the fact of death. Preachers do not often speak of the subject. The volumes of sermons on death so common in the seventeenth and eighteenth centuries would look strange in the modern minister's bookshelves. With this there is a hesitation in talking of death to those who are about to die.

The Death of Those we Love

In two ways the reluctance is shown. One is our attitude towards the dying of other people, particularly of those we love, whose lives have been entwined with ours. The depth of sorrow which comes when a friend dies is well expressed by Tennyson in his *In Memoriam*. This was about a close friend but some of the most painful experiences have come when a husband or wife has died. This has been vividly dealt with by C. S. Lewis in *A Grief Observed*, which was first published under the pseudonym N. W. Clerk, and later in Lewis's own name after he himself had died. In the book he set down his reflections on his wife's death. Physical pain was there. 'Nobody ever told me that grief felt so like fear. I am not afraid, but the sensation is like being afraid.' He talks of how distant God seems, and of the varying moods of those first days, but he accepts that death had to come, and concludes, 'How wicked it would be, if we could, to call the dead back!'[89]

This is the time when many are concerned not only

with the death of the one who was loved but with their own loss, and often they cannot really believe that husband or wife will not be seen again. Some fly to Spiritualism; others blame everyone, including the doctors, and in the end God himself. Even when the person who died was very old or was suffering dreadful pain, they will not accept that for all there is a time to die, and that includes the loved one. For many, perhaps the first step towards healing is this acceptance.

Mourning

I have come more and more to realise that there is, after a death, a season of mourning. Here also there is a kind of rhythm and it is often unwise to make decisions, eg concerning a new home, new friends, new places where to live, too quickly. Those who have witnessed the death of their partners and friends know that there are anniversaries to be remembered, birthdays, wedding days, perhaps children's birthdays. Each of these will bring a painful, if happy, reminder of the wife or husband, the parent, child or friend, and if each reminder is made an occasion of gratitude there is more likely to be a gradual healing.

The season of mourning is often made bearable by the help of friends and all of us can help sustain others in this way. Writing of the death of his wife, David Niven, who later was to fight so brave a battle with disease, said:

> I don't know how people can get through periods of great tragedy without friends to cushion and comfort them. To be alone in the world when disaster strikes must be an unbearable refinement of the torture, and I will ever bless those who helped me over the initial shock.[90]

Many would echo that, and for some, in addition to individual friends, there has been the affectionate fellowship of the church which has helped them through the lonely hours; but it is not always so, and for some mourners the loneliness of their grief is very bitter. And for all there

79

comes the time when human friends cannot be with them, when the widower goes home wanting to tell his wife all that has been happening and she is not there! David Niven also described that experience. 'But there comes a time when friends have to get on with their own lives and you have to face the problem alone . . . this is the worst part.' Yes, that is the testing time.

It is here that some find their Christian faith upholding them, though it is not always so. It is infinitely sad to see anyone who was strong in the faith crumbling when someone near has died, and sometimes turning away from God. The task of the Church is a delicate but necessary one to show understanding love. Equally I have known those whose faith never seemed very strong but who so faced the change that faith was deepened. They knew that the one who had died was in God's keeping and they trusted him for the future. One of the greatest upholding factors is the conviction that death is not the end. New life, new rhythms are opening. The man or woman, old person or child whom we loved still lives in the presence of God.

We Must All Die

It is this that brings me to the second way in which we are reluctant to face the fact of death. I write now of our own death. We are not immortal in the sense that we shall live for ever with no break, no change. Indeed the Christian does not believe in the natural immortality of the soul but in the resurrection of the body, the whole being, whereby God raises up those who have died an earthly death, so that the eternal life they have known here is brought to a greater fulness in him. Death is the gateway to life, as is so often declared on the gates and doors of crematoria, *Mors Janua Vitae*.

As men and women grow older the certainty of their own death comes home to them. Often it is a sudden realisation—'Somebody's walking over my grave!' Sometimes it is a gradual conviction, as they find themselves thinking of death. If physically life is miserable, if they have no joy in close friendships, they may find themselves longing for death, and who would wish to say that they are wrong? For the majority, however, I suspect that there is a natural hanging on to life, with a feeling that there is still much to be enjoyed, and they would not easily go along with Paul when he said: 'I am hard pressed between the two. My desire is to depart and be with Christ, for that is far better. But to remain in the flesh is more necessary on your account.'[91] Possibly he could so write because he was a bachelor. More seriously, he was so much more closely united to Christ than we. Whatever be people's attitude to words like that the truth is that death must come and they need to be prepared.

It is often said that the belief in life after death is one of the most difficult beliefs for Christians, as for others. Enquiries which are made from time to time about the convictions that Christians hold suggest that a majority do not believe that any form of life follows this present form. Among those who accept belief in resurrection there are varying views and difficulties in expression. I can only share a personal conviction. To me it is absurd to think of death as ending all. It does not make sense. But I cannot rely on that natural feeling alone. I believe that there is sound philosophy behind such a conviction and many thinkers, Christian and non-Christian, believe in a life after death. Most of all, however, I believe because Jesus believed, and because he himself went through death to the greater life of the resurrection, so that it was natural for the early Christians to have, as one of their most cherished convictions, 'Christ is alive'; and they lived in him.

Life After Death

Of the nature of that life we know but little. Some have described heaven and hell in great detail, owing more to Dante and Milton than to the Bible. We need to get away from the physical pictures so often painted, though we shall inevitably think in terms of people and of meeting those we knew here, and even more of seeing God face to face. It will not be a repetition of this life. Jesus said little about the nature of the hereafter, but he did make clear to the Sadducees who were trying to catch him out that it would not be just a continuation of this present life. To the question, 'Whose wife will she be?' when a woman had married seven brothers who had all died, he said plainly, 'In the resurrection they neither marry nor are given in marriage, but are like the angels in heaven.[92] This will be a new season, the life of all life, the completion of the rhythm begun on earth.

A year ago I shared in a reading party of ministers considering the question of the future life. We studied together the Drew Lectures which had been selected by the late Dr Charles Duthie, in a volume *Resurrection and Immortality*. Our study led us further. In particular I found help in Hans Küng's *Eternal Life*, and in a much simpler book, *A Time to Die*, by William Purcell.[93] We were naturally led to face again the fact of death and what our faith has to say. We were also helped to look at our ministry to the bereaved and there came to us the quiet certainty that what might seem to be the end of all seasons was in fact the beginning of something more wonderful. Wrote Christina Rossetti:

> We know not when, we know not where,
> We know not what that world will be,
> But this we know: it will be fair
> To see.
>
> With heart athirst and thirsty face
> We know and know not what shall be;
> Christ Jesus bring us of his grace
> To see.
>
> Christ Jesus bring us of his grace
> Beyond all prayers our hope can pray,
> One day to see him face to face—
> One day.

And here is an anonymous verse:

> When I was young I read,
>   'Blest are the dead,
> For they have passed to their eternal rest.'
> When I was old I said,
>   'Blest are the dead,
> For they shall work again, and work is blest.'[94]

The Man for all Seasons

Here was a man who was born in an obscure village, the child of a peasant woman. He worked in a carpenter's shop until he was thirty, and then for three years he was an itinerant teacher.

He never wrote a book. He never held an office. He never owned a home. He never had a family. He never went to college. He never travelled two hundred miles from the place where he was born. He had no credentials but himself. He had nothing to do with this world except the power of his divine manhood.

While he was still a young man the tide of popular opinion was turned against him. His friends ran away. One of them denied him. He was turned over to his enemies. He went through the mockery of a trial. He was nailed upon a cross between two thieves. His executioners gambled for the only piece of property he had on earth when he was dying—his coat. When he was dead he was taken down and laid in a borrowed grave through the pity of a friend.

Nineteen wide centuries have come and gone. Today he is the centre-piece of the human race and the leader of the column of progress.

I am far within the mark when I say that all the armies that ever marched, and all the navies that ever were built, and all the parliaments that ever sat, and all the kings that ever reigned, put together, have not affected the life of man upon this earth as powerfully as has— *that one solitary figure.*   Phillips Brooks

Dear Master, in whose life I see
All that I would, but fail to be,
Let thy clear light forever shine,
To shame and guide this life of mine.
John Hunter, *Congregational Praise* No 462

Firstly and lastly, everything rests upon this simple decision (about Christ); to cast in one's lot with him, to dare to believe that he was right about God, life and men, and though the heavens fall to be standing with him, living for him and dying with him. It is then we discover that the promises are true and know that the life which was in him is being manifested in us. We are not saved from perplexity, but we are saved from despair.

When I was young I had a lot to say about the Gospel and the Faith and Christian Doctrine and the Church. As I grow older I find I have only one thing to say, one name to speak, and only one to whom I can point. It is he, Jesus of Nazareth.
Leslie Cooke, *Bread and Laughter*

TEN

The Man for all Seasons

You will recall the title of a play about the life of a great Christian, Sir Thomas More. It was *A Man for all Seasons*. I take that description now and apply it to Jesus Christ, whom I would describe as 'The Man for all Seasons', for I believe that he has something to say to all the experiences through which men and women pass.

First I would like to say something about the difficulty which many may feel when called to follow Jesus, and to see him as one who can help in all seasons. How can he understand the life of a slum child as well as that of a public schoolboy? What can he do for an oppressed black African as well as for a free-living American? He was not married, he did not know the struggle some have to make ends meet, he was not unemployed (though some might question that, since he seems to have given up the safe job in the family business to become a wandering preacher, with nowhere to lay his head). His background was in many ways so different from ours. He was a man of one nation, a Jew. How can he speak to the Gentile world, to the people of China, India, Africa, the South Seas, Europe, America, Russia?

It would not have been possible for him to have all these experiences. To be human as well as divine he had to be a person of a particular sex, in one country, in one century, and with one kind of background, but that did not prevent him from having a deep sympathy with a Roman centurion, with a Samaritan leper, with those blind from birth, with the women who helped him and wept over him. Nor does it mean that he cannot be thought of as having something to say to the twentieth century as well as to the first. In him there is the kind of understanding which is seen in people who are able to help others who have widely different experiences. It is certainly true of many ministers. I agree with those who maintain that it is good that candidates for the ministry should generally have some experience other than that of students, and I have been grateful for those who advised me to spend time in business before entering college. In part this allows the testing of the call to minister by living and working with people of different backgrounds and it is a help to have had another job, as farm labourer, office worker, teacher, etc. It all means a broadening of experience. But it does not follow that all must take this course and I have known ministers from middle-class backgrounds who moved from school to university and on to theological college who have proved that they could minister to people in all walks of life, to the labourer as well as to the academic, to the rich as to the poor, to the Papuan or Hindu as well as to the country or city dweller in this country. It was possible because they had a real imaginative sympathy which enabled them to be at home with people of many races and ways of living, a sympathy which developed with the years. They went out towards other people, and therefore they were men and women for all seasons.

Jesus and the Seasons

The more we know of Jesus the more likely we are to have this kind of sympathy for all sorts and conditions of men and women, for it is a fact that people of varying races and social conditions find that he speaks to their situation. In these days of confrontation when the gap between nations and peoples often seems to be growing he is listened to by those who have different political views and philosophies. He became one not simply with individuals but with the whole human race. He may be thought of as having the qualities of spring, summer, autumn and winter. Go through the four seasons as outlined in chapter 2 and see in them this echo of Jesus' own life. He can also be thought of as the day and the night. In the Gospels he is seen as travelling, teaching, healing, preaching, in the light and clarity of the day and also he is watching, praying and resting, he was tried and condemned, in the night season.

In the seasons of the Christian Year he is also presented and all the aspects which the various observances emphasise are needed. He comes to us in the promise of Advent, as a child and in the Lenten days of temptation. He is seen at Easter in all his Resurrection glory, and he comes again through the Holy Spirit. This is the same Jesus through whom we see the Father also. Every aspect of Christian belief, every season of the faith, comes to us in him.

There are bound to be times when he seems to be remote from our own lives. To some indeed he has seemed as a stranger and an enigma. To others his life is transparent and they feel they know him right well. The truth will lie somewhere between both. Jesus will always have about him something of the mystery as well as the clarity of the changing seasons, but through the study of the gospels and the other New Testament writings, through the story of the Christian Church, and through the deep personal experiences of Christians throughout the centuries there comes home the increasing certainty that he is the man for all seasons. The refusal to accept this may well come from a self-pity which refuses to believe that anyone else has had such a hard time as the one concerned. As we journey along the roads with Christ we discover different facets of his nature and teaching. In the fourth century Ephrem Syrus, a great scholar of the Church, wrote of the woman who met Jesus at the well,[95] and how she responded to him:

> At the beginning of the conversation Jesus did not make himself known to her ... but first she caught sight of a thirsty man, then a Jew, then a Rabbi, afterwards a prophet, last of all the Messiah. She tried to get the better of the thirsty man, she showed her dislike of the Jew, she heckled the Rabbi, she was swept off her feet by the prophet, she adored the Christ.

The Man for all Ages

It is perhaps in looking at the way in which people of all ages feel that Jesus is speaking to them that he may most clearly be seen as a man for all seasons. When I think of him it is not just as one who is ageless, any more than I think of him as raceless. I see him growing up, as the babe of Bethlehem and as the boy in the temple; as the 'young prince of glory' (as so first of all described by Isaac Watts in his hymn *When I survey the wondrous cross*), and as a man of maturity. We need to keep in mind that in some respects the lifespan was shorter than it is now, and that childhood was briefer, so that girls and boys matured earlier. When Jesus was crucified he was more of middle age, as his contemporaries would have seen it. Moreover, his experiences made him seem older than he was. When he was only about thirty years old the Jews spoke of him as 'not yet fifty years old'.[96] Already he was bearing the burdens of the world.

I owe much to the ministry of John Patten, who moved from the church where I grew up to become Literary Superintendent of the British and Foreign Bible Society, and especially to a book of sermons by him entitled *Simon Peter's Ordination Day.* In one sermon he raised and answered the question:

> How old is Jesus? He is your age, young man. He stands by your side on the threshold of manhood, looking out on the world with eager and expectant gaze, sharing your fondest hopes and highest ambitions. How old is Jesus? He is your age . . . , you who are now in middle life, and he knows your special cares and anxieties. . . . He is as old as you [who are] bowed down with the years and frail through lessening strength. He will be the companion of your eventide. How old is Jesus? He is the age of everyone who receives him. He is the contemporary of the child, the youth, the man, the aged. Old with those who have seen much of life and its sorrows, he is eternally young to the new generation as it rises up to meet him.[97]

I would expand that. At any time you will find in him the qualities of different ages—the trustfulness and simplicity of the child, the readiness to adventure of the young, the steadiness of those who are middle-aged and the experience of the old. Moreover I would go through the experiences of life set out in chapters 5 to 9, for in those seasons I find in him an understanding and challenge and help that I need.

The Wide Experience of Jesus

The life of Jesus was to our way of thinking a brief one. His public ministry was concentrated into three years. Yet somehow he seems to have packed into that time the experiences of a long lifetime.

Jesus was one who was continually giving. Virtue went out of him as he gave healing to the sufferers yet he was one who gladly received. How happily he accepted the hospitality of friends like Lazarus, Mary and Martha, and the ministry of the women who journeyed with him, and how grateful he was for the companionship of his disciples: 'You are those who have continued with me in my trials'.[98] Of the action of the woman who anointed his head with a costly ointment and who was blamed for wasting what might have been sold and given to the poor, Jesus approved, recognising that she was with him in his sufferings and promising that 'wherever the gospel is preached in the whole world, what she has done will be told in memory of her'.[99] So it has been. Jesus gave lavishly and received generously.

Again, there were times when it seemed that Jesus was one who destroyed. He broke down some of the accepted beliefs of his day, showing the inadequacies of the faith and practice of the religion of his contemporaries. Consequently some have seen in him a rebel. That is only to touch on one aspect. Far more he was a creative thinker and a builder up of real faith. He showed a God of love as none had seen him before.

Jesus also lived in a time when there were war and peace. Hatred of the Roman Empire still moved the Jewish leaders and there are echoes of warfare throughout the gospels. Yet as far as Jesus was concerned he had come to wage only one war, the war against evil, the battle that went on inside the human heart. It is words of peace that we remember most from him, a peace much deeper than the peace imposed by the Emperor Augustus when Jesus was a young man. John Buchan vividly contrasts Jesus with the deified Roman ruler:

When the news of the death of the master of the world came to the Galilean hills, and the neighbours were troubled lest this should mean the end of the Augustan peace and an orderly empire, (Jesus) did not seem greatly concerned, for his thoughts were on a different peace and another empire. Sixteen years later he was to proclaim a kingdom mightier than the Roman, and to tell of a world saved not by Man who became God but by God who became Man.[100]

Jesus has been called 'a man of sorrows and acquainted with grief'.[101] The words were taken from the picture of the suffering servant in Isaiah and applied to Jesus in later years. With all the joy he knew and shared Jesus experienced grief such as few have known. It was not only the pain from the sufferings inflicted upon him, the wilful misunderstanding, the lack of comprehension of his closest followers, the continual opposition of those he came to help, the arrest, the ill-treatment, the condemnation, flogging, scourging, crucifixion. These were bitter enough, though it must always be kept in mind that others have suffered even greater cruelty. To all that has to be added the sorrows of other people that he voluntarily accepted. His sympathy was so deep that he bore the sins and anguish of others, and it is in that sense that we can apply to him the words from Isaiah, 'Surely he has borne our griefs and carried our sorrows'.[102] Was there ever grief like unto his grief?

I need hardly add that Jesus faced death courageously, not minimising its pain and the sense of loss. Had it been possible he would have been spared the suffering. But he met death, passed through it, and has given to us an assurance that death is not the end.

As we look again at all these seasons, we find in him the Man for all Seasons and can sing:

Thou, O Christ, art all I want;
More than all in thee I find.[103]

The Seasons Come and Go

Eternal Ruler of the ceaseless round
   Of circling planets singing on their way;
Guide of the nations from the night profound
   Into the glory of the perfect day;
Rule in our hearts, that we may ever be
Guided and strengthened and upheld by thee.

J. W. Chadwick, CP 554

     I have learned
To look on nature, not as in the hour
Of thoughtless youth; but hearing often-times
The still, sad music of humanity,
Nor harsh nor grating, though of ample power
To chasten and subdue. And I have felt
A presence that disturbs me with the joy
Of elevated thoughts; a sense sublime
Of something far more deeply interfused,
Whose dwelling is the light of setting suns,
And the round ocean and the living air,
And the blue sky, and in the mind of man.

William Wordsworth,
Lines composed above Tintern Abbey

     Lord, I have time,
I have plenty of time,
All the time that you give me,
The years of my life,
The days of my years,
The hours of my days,
They are all mine,
Mine to fill quietly, calmly,
But to fill completely, up to the brim,
To offer them to you, that of their insipid water
Yoy may make a rich wine such as you made once in Cana of
    Galilee!

Michel Quoist, Prayers of Life

Look carefully then how you walk, not as unwise men but as
wise, making the most of the time, because the days are evil.

Ephesians 5:15, 16

ELEVEN

The Seasons Come and Go

It would be possible to continue writing on the theme of the Seasons. This can cover the whole of life just as we often use the word 'world' to suggest every aspect of living, public and private. I began with the dictionary definitions and have only touched upon the many kinds of seasons there indicated. The hunting season, the cricket or football season, the season as understood by the wealthy in their visits to the social life of London in the last century, all these are of interest but they are not universal in their application. It has been in the book of Ecclesiastes that I have discovered the seasons which affect us all and these I have tried to follow through. I have covered to some extent most of the seasons he mentions and now add a few comments on the others.

More from Ecclesiastes
'A time to cast away stones, and a time to gather stones together'
This sentence may be linked with the seasons of destruction and rebuilding, since the more obvious meaning accepted by some scholars is that it refers to the scattering of the stones of an old building and then collecting them for a new structure. Others think of it as speaking of the unfriendly act of scattering stones to make a field unproductive. This is touched on in Jesus' parable of the sower, when 'other seed fell on rocky ground, where it had not much soil, and immediately it sprang up since it had no depth of soil; and when the sun rose it was scorched, and since it had no root it withered away.'[104] The result was the same whether the ground was naturally rocky or the result of an unfriendly action. The second half of the statement would then refer to a kindly gathering together of the stones cast abroad, so making the ground fruitful. This represents then the

seasons we know when we try to hinder other people's living and those when we seek to aid positively, creatively, lovingly.

'A time to embrace, and a time to refrain from embracing'

This could have referred to the times when we must greet one another, and then presumably when we should ignore others or not act effusively. In the ways of the world this may seem to be a wise approach to others. I would prefer to take it at its face value. There is a time when we ought to express in action our welcome, our care and concern for others, and also a time when it is best to be a little withdrawn. Both seasons are necessary in our relationships. Often we fail others because we do not show affection. Much has been said and written about the importance of touch, and embracing represents the action that shows more than words how we feel. The arm around the shoulder will count far more than many words of sympathy to a friend who is grieving. But there are times also when we should withdraw, when embracing may lead to trying to press our views and ourselves upon those we wish to help. They must act for themselves if they wish to grow.

'A time to seek, and a time to lose'
'A time to keep, and a time to cast away'

I take these together although they are not exactly the same in meaning. The first refers to the acquisition of property contrasted with losing it. The second has in mind guarding what we have in contrast with throwing it away. This is a little different from giving and receiving of which I wrote in chapter 5. There are times when people tend to acquire, not just knowledge, not even wealth, but possessions which mean a great deal to them. See how the amount of furniture, books, ornaments, clothes, accumulates as the homes you occupy grow larger. When retirement comes and you enter a smaller house, when you no longer need so many things, the second part of each sentence operates, and it is not an easy way to take. I think of the over-burdened bookshelves and stored up records of the past, sometimes going back to schooldays, of ministers who have died. Possibly many of us need to reflect as we grow older that there is rightly a time to keep but also wisely a time to cast away.

'A time to rend, and a time to sew'

This most likely refers to the mourning customs of the time, and links with what I have already said about seasons of mourning. The rending of a garment was a sign of mourning. But mourning must not last too long and there is a time for sewing up, repairing the breach in life, facing the future without the physical presence of the one who was loved.

'A time to love, and a time to hate'

If what has been written about the attitude of Ecclesiastes to war and peace is accepted, then this saying is expressing the same belief on an individual level rather than on the national level. There was a time when it was right to love but there were also days when people seemed compelled to hate. Today these words could be treated in a metaphorical sense. There are times when we must love all people but also times when we must hate the evil things in life. In that sense a Christian must be a good hater. Yet hate can never be the first word and to talk of loving the sinner and hating the sin he commits is always dangerous and likely to lead to confusion. The more our religious faith is based upon Christ the more love will overcome hate. Dean Swift was one who often wrote cynically about life but behind the cynicism of one of his sayings is a depth of wisdom: 'We have just enough religion to make us hate, but not enough to make us love one another.'[105]

The Seasons and Ourselves

As we look at the seasons of nature and of personal living, can we for a moment imagine what the world would be like if there were no seasons coming and going, no variations, only one deadening sameness? Milton touched on it when he wrote, with his own blindness in mind:

Thus with the Year
Seasons return, but not to me returns
Day, or the sweet approach of ev'n or morn,
Or sight of vernal bloom, or summer's rose,
Or flocks, or herds, or human face divine.

Yet Milton knew that in a richer sense even the blind
would know the seasons.

So much the rather thou Celestial light
Shine inward, and the mind through all her powers
Irradiate, there plant eyes, all mist from thence
Purge and disperse, that I may see and tell
Of things invisible to mortal sight.[106]

I knew a blind masseur who loved walking on the Sussex
Downs at all seasons. Sometimes I met him after he had
been out and he told with obvious delight how wonderful
was the scenery, how glorious the hills. He had experienced the seasons he could not see. If there were no
seasons we would make them.

So the seasons are alive, active. They may be thought
of as immediate, as specific points in time, or as the space
between those points. There will be shades of intensity in
all the seasons of life. I see this in the more personal
seasons of sorrow and joy; they may be brief but very
deeply felt, or they may be spread out, lasting a long
time. There are some seasons we wish could last for ever,
and indeed as we reflect they seem to have lasted longer
than in fact they did. For the most part, however,
whether brief or protracted, the seasons come and go;
there is movement.

As I look back over the seasons of varying nature, I see
that in one sense they follow one another, as summer
succeeds spring, joy follows weeping, building succeeds
to destruction. While writing this book I have continually
been hearing the tune and words of the musical *Fiddler on
the Roof*, and I must get them in before I close.

Sunrise—sunset; sunrise—sunset!
Swiftly fly the years.
One season following another,
Laden with happiness and tears.

96

We may often wish to jump some seasons but they follow each other inexorably.

That is not all that is to be said about the succession of seasons. It is not simply that one is added to another. Behind that succession I see a purpose being worked out. Not all can believe this. They can only see a succession, which gives order but no purpose. In his Preface to *A History of Europe* H. A. L. Fisher wrote:

> One intellectual excitement has, however, been denied me. Men wiser and more learned than I have discerned in history a plot, a rhythm, a predetermined pattern. These harmonies are concealed from me. I can only see one emergency following upon another as wave follows upon wave, only one great fact with respect to which, since it is unique, there can be no generalisations, only one safe rule for the historian: that he should recognise in the development of human destinies the play of the contingent and the unforeseen.[107]

I remember that when I first read those words I wondered how I in my ignorance dared question this judgment of a great scholar. However it is also true that many wise philosophers and learned historians do believe that there is a purpose displayed in history, as seen, eg in Herbert Butterfield's *Christianity and History*.[108] F. R. Barry, one of the foremost Christian writers of this century, writing after the years of war and change, said:

> I have lived to see nearly everything I care for and have spent my life trying to serve and set forward, suspect, derided and threatened with destruction. . . . I am no less perplexed than anyone else. Yet I can still, by the grace of God, believe in the truth of that faith by which I have tried to live. A New Testament writer wrote to . . . some hard-pressed converts about the shaking of all things that can be shaken, that the things which cannot be shaken may remain.[109]

Among those things he most surely would have believed was the purpose that was at the heart of the universe. It is more than 'one thing following another'.

97

God and the Seasons

So throughout the seasons, as they succeed each other and as we detect a purpose behind them and in them, we meet with God whose purposes are being worked out. This I tried to express in speaking of physical seasons. This we may discover in the seasons of our faith. He is the one who may become more real to us as we see him at work in our changing experiences, not only in happiness and success but in sorrow and in loss. All the seasons are in his hand.

It is indeed a part of his purpose to call upon us in all those seasons. Professor H. H. Farmer used to say that God never comes livingly to a man or woman without offering succour and making a demand. When I wrote of the Sombre Seasons I tried to suggest how God gives us help in our need. Yet all the way through he is asking something of us. It seems to me that while Jesus was bringing the Kingdom, declaring the Good News, he was also asking men and women to respond. One of his persistent calls was to follow him. He first called Peter and the other fishermen in what must have seemed to them to be the springtime in Galilee. It was simply 'follow me'.[110] It was as a summer day with warmth and the weariness of hard work when a scribe and another disciple offered to follow him, but wanted to make conditions.[111] How often would not the other followers have longed also to follow part of the way! It was as autumn when the shadows of the future were beginning to spread that he said to his disciples, 'If any man would come after me, let him deny himself and take up his cross and follow me.'[112] It was a time for counting the cost, as the young man found when Jesus said to him, 'If you would be perfect, go, sell what you possess and give to the poor, and you will have treasure in heaven; and come, follow me'.[113] It was winter in Peter's soul when, on the night of Jesus' arrest, trial, condemnation, the night before the Crucifixion, he followed his Master 'at a distance'.[114] In that winter all seemed lost when the body of Jesus was laid in a stranger's tomb but spring came again, and in the glory of the Resurrection Peter and his friends were once more by the side of the lake, after Jesus had spoken to them while fishing. Once more he talked specially with Peter, now by his side and remembering with thanksgiving and regret all that had passed but hearing again, as Jesus even spoke to him of the death he would die, the familiar demand, 'Follow me'. In one way Peter still hesitated and looked at another disciple and asked, 'Lord, what about this man?' And again Jesus told Peter that it was to him he was speaking as he said once more, 'Follow me'. It is you who are to follow.[115]

The seasons speak to us all and in them we hear continually that call. Who has put it more movingly than Albert Schweitzer?

He comes to us as One unknown, without a name, as of old by the lakeside he came to those men who knew him not. He speaks to us the same word: 'Follow me', and sets us the tasks which he has to fulfil for our time. He commands. And to those who obey him, whether they be wise or simple, he will reveal himself in the toils, the conflicts, the sufferings which they shall pass through in his fellowship, and, as an ineffable mystery, they shall learn in their own experience who he is.[116]

For Reflection and Discussion

1. For Everything a Season

Is everything planned for us in advance, so that the 'times' of which Ecclesiastes wrote are fixed and unalterable?

Set down a few guidelines for when to keep silence and when to speak.

2. The Rhythm of Life

Which is your favourite of the four seasons of the year, and why?

Do you detect a rhythm in your own life? What are the important elements in that rhythm?

Think about the dangers of being too much a creature of habit.

3. Seasons of Faith

Should we observe the Christian Calendar? Which are the seasons of the Christian Year which must be kept by all Christians?

What can we say to anyone who claims to be unable to accept the Christian faith?

4. Seasons That Come Not Again

How can you 'be your age'? Do you want to?

Read again what Hunter Davies says about Wordsworth in chapter 4, p 41. In what sense can the young person still be inside the middle-aged body?

Could you make out a case for euthanasia for those who are helpless and ready to die?

Think about the advice you would wish to give to those about to retire.

5. Giving and Receiving

Do you agree that it is more blessed to give than to receive?

Make a list of some of the gifts you have received which you regard as important. Make a list also of the important ways in which you have been able to give. Have you lost more than you have gained?

6. Breaking Down and Building Up

Are there things in the life of your church which need to be broken down? How would you replace what is destroyed?

Think about the causes of the breakdown of people's Christian faith. How can faith be rebuilt?

7. War and Peace

Is War ever justified? What defence policy could overcome it?

Consider the causes of violence in the world today, asking if terrorism is ever justified.

Were there times when you should have been angry, and you kept quiet?

8. Sombre Seasons

Are Christians too concerned with sorrow and the painful aspects of life?

Think about the part that Christian faith can play in the face of deep and prolonged depression. (The Fontana paperback *Depression* by Jack Dominian would help to provide a background to this.)

9. A Time to Die

How should funerals be conducted and mourning observed? Do the present arrangements declare the Christian faith about death and the future?

What happens at death? How do you picture the after-life?

102

10. The Man for All Seasons

It is sometimes said that Jesus cannot speak to all sorts and conditions of men and women because he could not have experienced every kind of life. Can you suggest any people and situations where he cannot help?

How do you think of Jesus? If you could paint his portrait or write a description, what would you emphasise? What adjectives would you use in describing him?

11. The Seasons Come and Go

Think over what Dean Swift had in mind when he said, 'We have just enough religion to make us hate, but not enough to make us love one another.'

Is there a purpose in life? If so, what is it?

Does Jesus still call men and women to follow him? Consider what it would mean today.

Some Prayers in Season and Out of Season

I first thought that I would write a prayer for every kind of season mentioned in the book, but quickly realised that this was too ambitious! So I decided to write a few prayers in the hope that the reader would be encouraged to write others.—R. J. H.

Too Much Rhythm

Lord God,

Sometimes it seems that there is too much rhythm in our lives; everything is so predictable. The seasons roll round, day follows night, week succeeds to week; even years we call new are like those we think of as old. At times we hear the same old story, and we wonder if there is anything to be known that is new.

Help us to see the value of the regular rhythm of life and also to discover the adventure hidden in the heart of repetition. May we expect that no days, weeks, seasons and years will be just as they were. By this time tomorrow may some new experience have been added to our lives.

On a Winter's Day

Dear Lord,

It is cold and wet; we have had fog and we fear the coming of snow. The days are too short and we do not feel like going out in the evening.

Thank you for the winter with all its cold and hardship. We were so glad to be out of doors in the summer, and anxious to keep summer as long as possible in the autumn, and to get all the outdoor jobs done before winter days.

Show us now how to enjoy these days. Sometimes we

shall remember the warmth of the summer as we look at postcards and photographs of those days; the golden glory of the autumn is not far away but we shall now be grateful for the new opportunities to be quiet, to meet our friends, to watch the television, to read old and new books, and to plan to help other people.

As we wonder at the quietness of nature we pray for all that lies beneath the soil, for trees and hills, to us sometimes seeming dead but preparing for the new life to come next spring.

A Sunday Prayer

We feel today is different, Lord. We are not as rushed as usual; we have time to talk to one another. Yet this is still a day of habit. We are going to church. We look forward to this and ask your blessing upon the preacher and the music. Thank you for all the preparation that has been made. May the word come alive for us. We admit that sometimes we find worship dull; we acknowledge that sometimes that is our own fault; but if there is a lack of liveliness in preacher and in singing we know you will still speak to us in the words of Bible and hymns and in the fellowship of Christian people.

The day is different but we cannot separate it from Saturday and Monday, and we ask your guidance upon this day of worship as on the days of business.

A Leisure-time Prayer

Dear God,

I have nothing special to do today; I am on holiday from my usual work. I know that the day may pass too quickly and that I can waste it as I have wasted so many days before. Help me to use this leisure well.

There are jobs to be done in the home and garden;

there are letters I have been meaning to write for months;

there are friends I should visit and other people who could be cheered by an unexpected call;

there are books I began to read but have not been able to finish.

I'm overwhelmed. Show me what is important and in all my activities help me also to relax, and to be still and know that you are God.

Perpetual Good Friday

We are thinking, Father, of the terrible sufferings of Jesus on the first Good Friday. Help us to remember the pain of the trial, the lifting up of the cross, the hours of exposure, the moment when it seemed that you had deserted him; and as in our minds we see all this, we also recall the suffering of your children throughout the centuries and today, suffering often equally undeserved and prolonged, suffering by which we ourselves live.

Yet we also remember the range of the life of Jesus, how he came as a child and brought great happiness to his parents and to the world. We recall the years of his childhood and his life in his home, and especially give thanks for the brief years of his ministry and the healing, wisdom, joy and peace they gave to us.

We know that the sorrow of the day was not simply defeat and that his love conquers. In his forgiveness we see enmity vanquished. Though he will die, Easter Day soon comes. We thank you that you brought him back from the dead and that he never dies again. May all the suffering of the world lead to a new resurrection.

For Those who are Sure

Lord God,

We pray today for those who are confident in their faith and are sure that nothing will disturb it. It isn't like that with us. Our lives are often clouded by doubt, limited by uncertainty, weakened because we are not sure of ourselves as well as you.

Bless those who have a strong faith. May they be able humbly to share it with others. May their faith mature with the passing years.

Keep together in love those who are sure and those who have doubts, that they may learn from each other and never judge one another harshly. In the happiness and

107

pain that may come to us all, give us humility and the joy of Christ's presence.

For Those who are Depressed

God of all experiences,

We are praying for those who suffer from deep depression. We know that this is more serious than our own times when we are miserable, anxious, afraid, for in our hearts we believe that such seasons will pass. Our concern is for those who remain so depressed that nothing cheers them, for whom the sun of joy seems to be obliterated, and faith and hope count for nothing. We do not understand them; we feel so helpless.

We pray for doctors who seek to help them and for all the skills they bring.

We pray for their families and friends who suffer with them that they may be given patience and continuing love.

And we ask that we ourselves may never give them up. May we have the right words to speak and the action which will declare our love. In the darkness of their depression may they meet with you.

A Prayer from Retirement

I find it difficult, Jesus, to accept that the business that held me for so many years controls my time no longer and that I am free from so many ties and responsibilities. Sometimes I resent it and feel slighted that they are getting along quite well without me. Forgive my pride.

People are finding jobs for me to do and I want to help but I am retired!

I want also in these years that are given to me to grow. Make me a more understanding person; help me to encourage those who are as busy as I was once. May I take up some of the ideas and thoughts I once had but have been too busy to pursue since I was younger.

Let me find time to deepen my friendships and to learn more about you, to pray for others as well as for myself, and to prepare for the great adventure of the life beyond this life.

A Time to Die

Lord of all my days,

I hesitate to speak about this, even to pray about it, and I don't want to sound miserable but I ask you to help me to accept that in your wisdom this life I now live is but a beginning, an entry into a life that is far beyond anything I can understand.

I have loved this life, the world of nature, the seasons of the year, the friends around me, the fun and also the sadness that have been mine, the work that has been done; and I know that others will miss me when I die.

Thank you for showing me in Christ that our human death will never separate us from your love. I do not know when my time to die will come, and if there is to be suffering beforehand, give me courage; especially save me from hurting those who love me and will have their own sorrow.

In the meantime, since I do not know the time of death, help me to accept the eternal life Christ gives me now and to be ready for whatever may happen.

Jesus the First and the Last

Lord Jesus, sometimes I cannot accept all that is said about your being the Man for all Seasons, the first and the last. I have tried to keep so much of my life from you. There are areas where I would like to think you have nothing to say to me.

I cannot really hide myself. You continually break through. You were there when I was a child; that was not hard to accept. In my youth though I wandered I could not escape you, and however busy I was in later years you continually reminded me of your presence and care. I have always seen you as of my own age, and in cheerfulness and sadness you have been my companion, ever beckoning me to greater heights.

I need to know you better. Show me your humanity, reveal to me your oneness with the Father. May I see you in the life of the world, in its victories and defeats. May the lessons that I once learned be overtaken by the wonders you have still to show me.

109

NOTES

Chapter One

1. William Neil's *One Volume Bible Commentary* (Hodder & Stoughton) p 242.
2. R. C. Walton (Ed) *A Basic Introduction to the Old Testament* (SCM) p 167.
3. C. S. Knopf, *The Optimism of Koheleth.* Quoted with approval by M. A. Eaton, *Ecclesiastes,* p 78. 'Koheleth' (or 'Qoheleth') is the Hebrew title, often translated 'The Preacher' but it means probably 'one who gathers an assembly to address it'.
4. J. P. de Caussade, *Spiritual Instruction on Prayer.*
5. Ecclesiastes 5:2.
6. Ecclesiasticus (Ben Sirach) 20:7, 8.

Chapter Two

7. Norman Goodall, *One Man's Testimony* (Independent Press), p 89.
8. James 5:7.
9. W. B. Yeats, *The Tower.*
10. *Four Seasons*—An Anthology chosen by E. Phelps and G. Summerfield (OUP).
11. Op. cit., p 57.
12. W. W. How, CP 644.
13. John Keats, *To Autumn.*
14. S. Longfellow, CP 653.
15. Coventry Patmore, *Winter Poems.*
16. Gordon Manley, *Climate and the British Scene* (W. Collins).
17. Hebrews 4:10, but read the whole chapter.
18. John Oman *The Office of the Ministry.*
19. Thomas Ken, CP 617.
20. G. D. Stewart, *The Lower Levels of Prayer* (SCM), p 70.

Chapter Three

21. Alfred Tennyson, *In Memoriam.*
22. Ephesians 4:12, 13.

23. Matthew 11:28, 29.
24. For information about the beginning and history of the Christian Calendar and Seasons, consult the appropriate articles in Hasting's *One Volume Dictionary of the Bible.*
25. Charles Dickens, *A Christmas Carol.*
26. See Exodus 34:28; 1 Kings 19:8; Matthew 4:2.
27. From a poem by Dora Greenwell, often quoted by Dr S. Cave, of New College.
28. Romans 6:9.
29. Harriet Auber's hymn, CP 209.
30. H.K. Moulton, *The Challenge of the Concordance*, p 102. Reprinted by permission of Marshall Pickering.
31. Robert Browning, *Pippa Passes.*
32. Alfred Tennyson, *In Memoriam.*

Chapter Four

33. Quoted in *Documents Illustrative of the History of the Church* (Ed B. J. Kidd), from Hegesippus *c.* 160-80.
34. See John 7:5; 1 Corinthians 15:7, where the reference is to James, the Brother of our Lord; Galatians 1:19 and 2:9. Cp Acts 12:17; 15:13; 21:18.
35. T. S. Eliot, *Little Gidding.*
36. Augustine, *Confessions.* Translation by R. S. Pine-Coffin (Penguin Classics).
37. From a sermon preached at Brighton, 12th August 1849.
38. Psalm 90:10.
39. Letter from *A Religious Rebel* (Ed L. Pearsall Smith), p 156.
40. L. J. Tizard, *Facing Life with Confidence.*
41. An echo from Philip Sidney's *Apologie for Poetrie.*
42. Hunter Davis, *William Wordsworth*, pp 172, 174. Used by permission of Weidenfeld & Nicholson.

Chapter Five

43. Acts 20:35.
44. 1 Corinthians 4:7. Cp Romans 5:15-17.
45. Helen Keller, *The Story of my Life.* Reprinted by permission of Hodder & Stoughton Ltd.
46. John 21:18.
47. 1 Thessalonians 2:8.
48. Romans 1:11, 12.

49. Ursula Gwynn, *The Green Hill.*
50. Author unknown. This is often sung as a hymn in the USA.

Chapter Six

51. M. A. Eaton, *Ecclesiastes* (Inter-Varsity Press), p 79.
52. E. C. Hoskyns and N. Davey, *The Riddle of the New Testament* (1931), p 24.
53. Edmund Gosse, *Father and Son* (Evergreen, 1941), p 9.
54. 1 Samuel 15:3, 18.
55. Matthew 5:43, 44.
56. Luke 14:28-30.

Chapter Seven

57. 2 Samuel 11:1.
58. Isaiah 2:4; Micah 4:3.
59. Luke 14:31-33.
60. James 4:1.
61. John 14:27.
62. Ephesians 2:14.
63. Revelation 12:7.
64. T. Hughes, CP 522.
65. Mark 3:1-6.
66. H. E. Fosdick, *The Manhood of the Master,* p. 36. Quoted by permission of the author and SCM Press Ltd.
67. Jonah 4:4.
68. Ernest Renan, *La Réforme Intellectuale et Morale.*
69. *Scottish Paraphrases, 1781,* CP 322
70. Romans 13:1-4.
71. R.F. Horton, *An Autobiography* (Allen and Unwin).

Chapter Eight

72. A. C. Swinburne, *Hymn to Proserpine.*
73. Matthew 11:16-19.
74. John 15:11.
75. Chairman's Address, CUEW, 1952, *The Work of the Ministry.* Now printed in *Facing Life and Death* by Leslie J. Tizard. Reprinted by permission of Allen & Unwin Ltd.
76. Luke 19:41, 42.
77. H. H. Farmer, *Towards Belief in God,* Vol 1, p 98. Used by permission of SCM Press Ltd.
78. Matthew 26:75.

79. Matthew 27:3-5.
80. G. F. Bradby, *Through the Christian Year* (SCM).
81. Jeremiah 20:7ff.
82. Isaiah 38:9-19.
83. David Cecil, *The Stricken Deer* (Constable).
84. *Selected Letters of William Cowper* (J. M. Dent), Everyman Edition, p 50.
85. William Blake, *Auguries of Innocence.*
86. C. S. Lewis, *The Problem of Pain* (Geoffrey Bles, Centenary Press), pp vii, viii.
87. Author unknown; quoted by James Reid, *The Keys of the Kingdom.*

Chapter Nine

88. Ecclesiastes 9:10.
89. *A Grief Observed*, by C. S. Lewis (N. W. Clerk), publisher Faber & Faber.
90. David Niven, *Bring on the Empty Horses* (Hamish Hamilton), p 75.
91. Philippians 1:23, 24.
92. Matthew 22:23-33.
     Resurrection and Immortality, Ed C. S. Duthie (Samuel Bagster).
     Eternal Life, Hans Küng (Collins).
93. *A Time to Die*, William Purcell (Mowbrays).
94. *Through the Christian Year* (SCM).

Chapter Ten

95. John 4:7-30.
96. John 8:57.
97. J. A. Patten, *Simon Peter's Ordination Day* (James Clarke).
98. Luke 22:28.
99. Mark 14:3-9.
100. John Buchan, *Augustus*, 1941 edition, p 327. Used by permission of Rt. Hon. Lord Tweedsmuir.
101. Isaiah 53:3.
102. Isaiah 53:4.
103. Charles Wesley, CP 473.

Chapter Eleven

104. Mark 4:5, 6.
105. Jonathan Swift, *Thoughts on Various Subjects.*

106. John Milton, *Paradise Lost*, Book III.
107. H. A. L. Fisher, *A History of Europe* (Edward Arnold), p.v.
108. See H. Butterfield, *Christianity & History* (G. Bell & Sons), final paragraph in chapter 5, p 112.
109. F. R. Barry, *To Recover Confidence*. Used by permission of SCM Press, Ltd.
110. Matthew 4:19.
111. Matthew 8:19-22.
112. Matthew 16:24.
113. Matthew 19:21.
114. Luke 22:54.
115. John 21:19-22.
116. The final words in Albert Schweitzer's *The Quest of the Historical Jesus*.

   CP—Congregational Praise.   NCP—New Church Praise.

ADDITIONAL ACKNOWLEDGEMENTS

Unless otherwise noted, the Scripture quotations contained herein are from the *Revised Standard Version* of the Bible, copyrighted 1946, 1952, 1971, by the Division of Christian Education of the National Council of the Churches of Christ in the USA, and are used by permission. All rights reserved.

Quotation from *New English Bible*, Second Edition © 1979 by permission of Oxford and Cambridge University Presses.

Osbert Sitwell's poem *Mrs Hague*, from Modern Verse, 1900-1940, Gerald Duckworth & Co. Ltd. Used by permisson.

Quotation from *Bread and Laughter* by Leslie Cooke. ©1986 World Council of Churches, Geneva. Used by permission.

HELPS TO FURTHER STUDY OF ECCLESIASTES

One Volume Bible Commentary, William Neil (Hodder & Stoughton). Written with lay preachers in mind.

Peake's *Commentary on the Bible*, Second Edition (Thomas Nelson & Sons).

Ecclesiastes, Commentary by Michael A. Eaton (Inter-Varsity Press).

Ecclesiastes, ICC Commentary by G. A. Barton (T. & T. Clark). More for the scholar.